3

D1367113

Penetrating the U.S. Auto Market
German and Japanese Strategies
1965-1976

Research for Business Decisions, No. 22

Gunter Dufey, Series Editor
Professor of International Business and Finance
The University of Michigan

Other Titles in This Series

Penetrating the U.S. Auto Market

German and Japanese Strategies
1965-1976

by
James Rader

umi
RESEARCH PRESS

JEROME LIBRARY-BOWLING GREEN STATE UNIVERSITY

Copyright © 1980, 1979
James Rader
All rights reserved

Produced and distributed by
UMI Research Press
an imprint of
University Microfilms International
Ann Arbor, Michigan 48106

Library of Congress Cataloging in Publication Data

Rader, James, 1950-
    Penetrating the U.S. auto market.

    (Research for business decisions ; 22)
    Bibliography: p.
    Includes index.
    1. Automobile industry and trade—United States.
2. Export marketing. 3. Automobiles, German.
4. Automobiles, Japanese. I. Title. II. Series.
HD9710.U52R28   382'.456292'0973   80-15530
ISBN 0-8357-1106-4

Contents

Contents

Figures

Figures

Tables

Tables

Tables

Tables

Acknowledgments

Many individuals contributed to completion of this research. I wish to express particular gratitude to the members of my dissertation committee: Professors Edward L. Wallace, C. Carl Pegels, and Vijay Mahajan. Professor Mahajan's keen methodological expertise, enthusiasm and constant encouragement animated and sustained the research effort. Professor Pegels offered understanding in the darkest moments and patiently endured my incessant questions. Always unselfish, he was always there when I needed help. My debt to Professor Wallace is large indeed. He introduced me to the literature of corporate strategy and made it live. As chairman of my doctoral committee, his was the guiding hand overseeing the research. He contributed an enormous amount of time and effort to the writing of this study, polishing, refining, and coordinating. I shall always be grateful for these efforts.

The early versions of this research were typed by Dolores Birchenough, who surrendered her holidays, nights, and weekends so that deadlines could be met. Figures, tables, and the final draft were proofread and typed by my sister, Jeanne Sandusky, who managed to handle an infant son concurrently. I am indebted to both these ladies for their unflagging ability to construct readable prose from my illegible scribbling.

The responsibility for any errors, shortcomings, or omissions in the text is entirely mine.

James Rader
Buffalo, New York
Fall, 1979

I

Introduction

The automotive industry is one of the largest and most important segments of the American economy. In 1975 the value of its production within the United States was over forty-five billion dollars, constituting three percent of the Gross National Product.[1] Over the past decade, direct production of automobiles has averaged approximately four percent of GNP.[2] Mere production, however, considerably understates the impact on the American economy of the domestic automobile industry. In 1976, worldwide, the four major American automobile producers sold ninety-four billion dollars worth of products, earning a net income of 4.26 billion dollars and employing almost one and one half million people,[3] of whom seven hundred and seventy-four thousand were employed in the U.S.[4] Further, these American jobs paid an average of one third better than the average United States wage level.[5] Consequently, successful penetration of the domestic automobile market by Japanese and German automakers constitutes a direct threat to the well-being of the American economy and the American labor force. This threat has been summarized by Henry Ford II, chairman of the Ford Motor Company, who states: "For every one percent of import penetration, there are twenty thousand fewer jobs available in the U.S."[6] At the penetration level of twenty percent achieved by foreign producers in April, 1977,[7] Mr. Ford's estimate amounts to a loss of four hundred thousand of these well-paid jobs to foreign economies.

Concentration on the automotive industry, however, ignores the wider implications of foreign automakers' penetration of the American market. In 1976, automotive imports into the United States contributed 16.4 billion dollars to the U.S. balance of payments deficit.[8] Moreover, at a time when the United States was attempting to limit imports of foreign steel, millions of tons of Japanese and German steel have entered the country in the bodies, frames and drivelines of imported automobiles, in addition to the aluminum, rubber, and plastics consumed in production of each foreign automobile. Each of these represents substantial lost sales to American industries deriving large proportions of their demand from domestic production of automobiles.[9,10]

Before any public or private American response to this foreign penetration of the domestic automobile market can be formulated, however, it is necessary to understand the phenomenon. This study is dedicated to furthering this necessary understanding through description, analysis, and evaluation of the marketing strategies employed by the strongest foreign participants in the American automarket: the Japanese and German manufacturers.

HISTORY OF FOREIGN PENETRATION
OF THE UNITED STATES AUTOMARKET

Foreign interest in the United States automarket is not a new phenomenon. It began in the years immediately following World War II when the British, traditional manufacturers to the world, attempted to establish themselves in the U.S. market. In the early fifties the British were joined by German producers who quickly displaced them as the major automobile importers. The level of penetration achieved by foreign manufacturers at this time was aptly described by Leslie Darbyshire in his 1957 dissertation[11] as "puny." During the period of his study, 1948 to 1955, the imports' deepest penetration of the American market was 200,000 units out of a total market of several millions.

In the years which followed, the advent of compact automobiles manufactured in the United States, and competitive pressure from the German automakers, gradually reduced sales of all foreign models, save those produced by Volkswagen and Mercedes, to the level of fringe competition. From the American automobile manufacturers' point of view, the United States continued to be a friendly market, absorbing ever increasing quantities of American products while turning a cold shoulder to foreign temptations. Lawrence Jay White in his 1969 dissertation on "The American Automobile Industry in the Postwar Period"[12] dismissed the prospects for foreign competition as "insignificant." As late as July of 1968 the Journal of Marketing published a paper[13] whose main theme was the need for American buyers of imported automobiles to overcome their feelings of dissonance resulting from the purchase of an unusual automobile, a foreign car. Consequently, scholarly research on the automobile industry during this period centered on American manufacturers. The topics of interest to a self-contained market were consumer purchase behavior,[14,15,16,17,18,19] overall demand forecasting,[20,21] and the prediction of market shares[22,23] in what had become a four power oligopoly led by the General Motors Corporation.

By the 1970's, however, a new nation entered the world automotive arena — Japan. Protected in its domestic markets by tariff and ownership restrictions,[24] Japan's automotive industry rose from the ashes of its prewar truck industry, increasing its production from 760,000 units in 1960 to 5.5 million units by 1970.[25]   Concurrent with this surge in domestic production, the number of Japanese auto manufacturers shrank from eleven to five,[26] thus removing domestic competition and allowing the remaining manufacturers to seize full advantage of large scale mass production technology. Having captured their home market, the largest Japanese producers, Toyota and Nissan, who had been fringe competitors in the United States since 1958 and 1959 respectively,[27] began their assault on the U.S. market. As Figures 1-1 and 1-2 show, from 1966 to 1973 their American sales rose from 50,000 to 650,000 units,[28] mostly at the expense of domestic producers. By April of 1977, Japanese and German firms held 15.8% of the total U.S. auto market, with the Japanese firms alone holding an 11.74% market share.   Meanwhile, American Motors, the weakest of the U.S. producers, saw its market share sink to 1.6%.[29]

IMPLICATIONS OF A LARGE IMPORT SHARE
OF THE UNITED STATES MARKET

The impact on the economy of a continued and growing Japanese and German presence in the American auto market reflects the importance of the automobile in the American lifestyle. The Census recorded an increase in "urban fringe" population from 21.1% of the U.S. population in 1960 to 26.8% of the larger U.S. population in 1970.[30] While the recent rise in energy prices may slow this trend, historical experience is definitely suburban in orientation. Moreover, competition from alternative modes of personal transport, promoted by both government and private organizations, has failed to move Americans from their cars onto public transport. At this time, no alternative mode has been discovered which the American people regard as a viable choice over their private automobiles.

The economic implications of a strong import presence in the U.S. domestic automobile market stem directly from the high level of fixed costs associated with automobile manufacturing. As White has noted,[31] an economical volume is achieved in the automobile industry only when hundreds of thousands of units are produced. Moreover, the American habit of yearly model revisions pushes each company's breakeven point still higher. American Motors Corporation, the weakest of American producers but still a world behemoth with 1976 sales of 2.3 billion dollars,[32] is currently losing money on passenger automobile production. Should AMC's market share slip below its current 1.6% (1976), losses may well drive AMC out of the domestic passenger automobile market as happened to Studebaker. Other producers, while not as threatened as AMC, face lost volume and lower profitability because of import pressure. Finally, there is the implication of reduced American ability to compete in foreign markets. Automobile markets now developing in the underdeveloped nations are potentially large and valuable. A strong home market position allows a company to maintain and enhance its economies of scale while penetrating foreign markets. To the extent that foreign producers succeed in reducing the American manufacturers' position in their domestic market, they weaken the ability of the American automobile manufacturers to successfully penetrate foreign markets, thus affecting both America's employment levels and balance of payments.

PURPOSE OF THE STUDY

The purpose of this study is to describe, analyze, and evaluate the strategies employed by the Japanese and German automakers in penetrating the American market.

The automotive industry is an extremely important component of the American economy. Domestic manufacturers have lost a large portion of this market to foreign competitors, the most successful of whom have been based in Japan or Germany. Therefore, any competitive effort to stem the tide of automotive imports must begin with an analysis of the strategies employed by the Japanese and German firms in achieving their penetration. Beyond this, however, the Japanese and German penetration of the American market for automobiles constitutes a case in which a mature industry in a technologically advanced nation was heavily penetrated by firms based in other technologically advanced nations. Study of Japanese and German penetration of the American market for automobiles will, therefore, give insight into patterns of competitive behavior which result when firms based in advanced countries compete in other technically sophisticated markets.

This purpose, to analyze the competitive behavior of two groups of strong foreign competitors in the American market, imposes three constraints on the breadth of the study. First, foreign firms based in countries other than Germany and Japan are specifically excluded. The study seeks to identify national differences among the automanufacturers who have taken strong positions in the American market. These are the Japanese and German firms. Inclusion of firms from other countries would blur any national distinctions between the competitive behavior of the German firms and that of the Japanese. Second, American manufacturers and their foreign subsidiaries are excluded. Corporate strategy flows from corporate goals. It is the purpose of this study to examine foreign companies' behavior in the American market. Domestic manufacturers and their foreign subsidiaries follow goals derived in the United States, not in other countries. Third, during the time period covered by this study, the firms examined produced all of their automobiles and acquired virtually all of their capital outside the United States. Moreover, the United States, while a large market, was only one of many foreign markets penetrated by these firms. Within the United States, their sole functional activity was marketing. Therefore, because it is the purpose of this analysis to study German and Japanese competitive behavior within the United States, only the firms' marketing strategies are included in the analysis.

OBJECTIVES

The study fulfills its purpose by addressing three specific research questions:

1. What strategies did the other German and Japanese automanufacturers, especially the Japanese, employ in ending Volkswagen's dominance of the U.S. market for imported automobiles?
2. Have Japanese firms and German firms, as groups, employed the same or different strategies in the U.S. auto market?
3. Have high volume firms employed a set of strategies that are significantly different from those of low volume firms?

Additionally, each firm's strategy is evaluated in terms of its success in the marketplace using both effectiveness and efficiency criteria. Finally, it is the nature of studies in corporate strategy to depart from basic hypotheses about corporate behavior in search of both the means of and reasons for that behavior. Consequently, this study has been alert to the possible discovery of unanticipated behavior and results which were not incorporated in the initial research questions.

Meeting these objectives required an extensive examination of the firms' marketing strategies with particular emphasis placed on the developmental aspects of these strategies. Because the quality of a firm's strategy is not an absolute, but rather a relative judgment, comparative analytical techniques were employed. Howard-Harris clustering was used to associate the firm's products in each year on the basis of similarity among their attributes. This allowed groups of product/markets to be identified, thus determining each firm's product/market scope and direct competitors. Discriminant analysis was used in addressing the specific research questions. This allowed direct comparison of the strategies employed by each of two groups of firms on a multidimensional basis. The search for unanticipated results employed correlation analysis in seeking relationships among the strategic dimensions and clustering to search for patterns among the firms' strategies.

The research questions were formulated with the expectation of certain results. Each specific question compares two dissimilar groups. The first sets Volkswagen, a firm which declined from market dominance to a position of comparative weakness, against the spectrum of generally prospering Japanese and German automakers. The second question opposes the Japanese and German manufacturers, national groups from opposite sides of the world. The third question compares the firms with high sales volume to those with substantially lower shares of the American market. In each case it was assumed that these dissimilarities in fortune, nationality, and depth of penetration would be reflected in the firms' strategies. However, no initial assumptions were made as to how or to what degree the strategies would differ. The search question was also formulated in the expectation of certain results. Consistent implementation of a strategy requires that a firm's positions on some strategic dimensions be related to positions on others and that these positions be altered concurrently when strategic changes are implemented. Therefore, concurrent changes in elements of each firm's marketing mix were anticipated. The second part of the search, the cluster analysis, was done to identify firms which were following similar strategies. These "strategic groups" have been identified in other industries.

STRUCTURE OF THE STUDY

There are three major structural elements of this study: literature, description of product/market scope, and analysis of the firms' overall marketing strategies. Chapter II contains a survey of the literature relevant to understanding the strategic behavior of the German and Japanese automanufacturers in the American market. This includes the theoretical literature underlying the concepts of corporate strategic analysis, as well as literature pertaining to marketing strategy, marketing strategy in multinational firms, and the impact of marketing strategy on profitablity. The chapter then proceeds to map the general concepts of strategic analysis onto the specific case of the German and Japanese automanufacturers.

Product/market scope is discussed in Chapter III. This chapter begins with a discussion of the concept of product/market scope and the interrelationship of product/market scope and marketing strategy. Each dimension of marketing strategy is defined in terms of one or more measurable variables which are grouped into sets of vectors for use in strategic analysis. A methodology for description of the firms' product/market scopes through analysis of their products' attributes is then developed and applied. Two sets of findings are reported: the overall pattern of development of product/market scopes among the German and Japanese automakers, and the development of each firm's individual product/market scope.

The third section of the book consists of analysis of the firms' overall marketing strategies. Differences in the strategies employed by Volkswagen and the other firms, between the two national groups of firms and between the higher sales volume and lower sales volume firms are reported in Chapters IV, V, and VI respectively. Chapter VII discusses interactions among the elements of marketing strategy. Groups of firms following similar strategies are identified and compared in Chapter VIII. Chapter IX reports each firm's relative degree of strategic success in penetrating the American market. Finally, Chapter X presents an integrated summary of the strategies employed by each German or Japanese firm and group of firms in the U.S., their relative success or failure, and directions for future research.

Two appendices are provided. Appendix A contains the within groups correlation matrices and Pearson product-moment correlation matrices generated in examination of relationships among strategic dimensions. Appendix B consists of a yearly breakdown of German and Japanese product/market groups and of a detailed identification of each firm's direct competitors on an annual basis.

The study, therefore, begins with a survey of the literature of corporate, marketing, and multinational strategies. Product/markets penetrated by the German and Japanese automakers are identified and each automaker's product/market scope is described. The American marketing strategies employed by each firm and group of firms are contrasted to discover differences in competitive behavior between national and volume groups and between Volkswagen and the other German and Japanese automanufacturers. Finally, the effectiveness and efficiency of each firm's penetration of the American market is evaluated to determine the firm's degree of strategic success.

Figure 1-1

Sales of Automobiles Within the United States

	Total Sales	Imported	$\dfrac{\text{Imports}}{\text{Total}}$ *100	Japanese & German Manufacturers	$\dfrac{\text{J\&G}}{\text{Total}}$ *100	$\dfrac{\text{J\&G}}{\text{Imports}}$ *100
1976	10111	1500	14.8	1277	12.6	85.1
1975	8640	1587	18.4	1216	14.1	76.6
1974	8867	1413	15.9	1065	12.0	75.4
1973	11439	1763	15.4	1402	12.3	79.5
1972	10950	1623	14.8	1263	11.5	77.8
1971	10250	1568	15.3	1211	11.8	77.2
1970	8405	1285	15.3	1011	12.0	78.7
1969	9583	1118	11.7	815	8.5	72.9
1968	9656	1031	10.7	742	7.7	72.0
1967	8337	769	9.2	566	6.8	73.6
1966	9028	651	7.2	500	5.5	76.8
1965	9332	569	6.1	412	4.4	72.4
	thousands	thousands	percent	thousands	percent	percent

Figure 1-2

Total Sales of Automobiles Within the United States

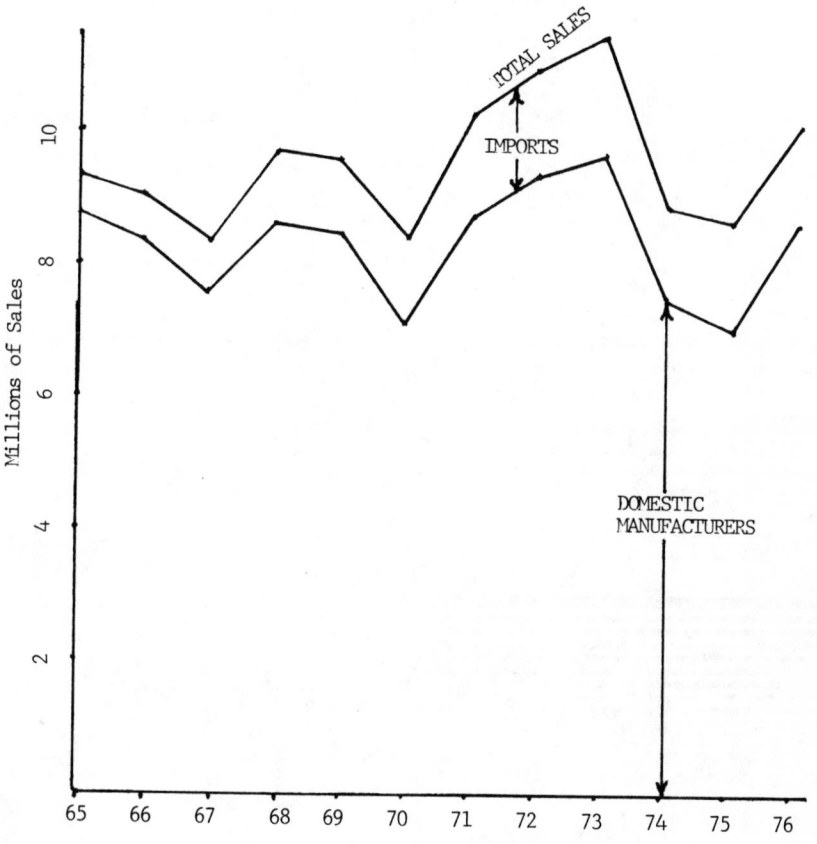

II

Strategy

The Japanese and German automanufacturers, the subjects of this study, are corporations owned and controlled in Japan or Germany which market their products in the United States. Three aspects of the literature of corporate strategy are relevant to a better understanding of their competitive behavior in the United States: the general literature of corporate strategy, the literature of multinational corporate strategy, and the literature of marketing strategy with the profitability implications of marketing strategy.

In this chapter the general literature of corporate strategy is explored with particular attention being given to its marketing aspects. The related concepts of a product/market and a firm's product/market scope are defined. Marketing strategy is shown to be a composite of a firm's competitive behavior among four dimensions: product, as reflected in the firm's choice of product/markets and product/market scope; price of its product line; distribution network; and promotional efforts.

Following this, there is a survey of corporate strategy considerations particularly relevant to multinational firms. This discussion focuses on marketing strategy, especially an analysis of similarities and differences in international markets and the strategic implications of possible variation in a firm's environment upon its marketing approaches across national boundaries. Legal, cultural, and commercial aspects are discussed and related to their possible impact on the corporation's overall strategy.

Finally, the chapter provides an overview of reasearch linking profitability to sales volume and the implications of this for a firm's choice of strategy. The literature reports a strong link betwen volume and profitability. Strategically, therefore, a profit-seeking firm must consider the impact of strategic choices on market share in determining its product/market scope.

STRATEGIC THEORY

There are almost as many definitions of the term "corporate strategy" as there are authors on the subject. Chandler[1] defines strategic decisions as those "concerned with the long term health of the enterprise." Russell Ackoff[2] states that a statement of strategy is characterized by its long-term, large-scale, goal-oriented nature. According to Jack Vance,[3] "corporate strategy . . . is the deployment of resources to achieve an objective." All of these authors have contributed to the overall description of corporate strategy as goal-oriented, long-term, wide in scope, and involving the allocation of resources.

However, this broad definition of corporate strategy, encompassing, as it does, the overall scope of the firm's activities, has engendered a widely divergent body of literature. This literature, however, centers about four major strategic issues:

1. Investigation of the relationship between a firm's strategy and its organizational structure,
2. Investigation of the relationship between a firm's strategic choice and its level of financial or marketing success,
3. Investigation of the information requirements of strategy formulation and of the sources used by managers in fulfilling these requirements, and
4. Investigation of the relationship between a competitive environment and the choice of a strategy to fit the environment.

One of the original fields of strategic research, studies of the relationship between strategic choice and organizational structure stems from Alfred Chandler's landmark 1962 investigation[4] of the evolution of many of the United States' largest enterprises. Chandler found that successful implementation of corporate strategy was inextricably linked to the development of an organizational structure capable of supporting the strategy. Recently, this area of research has been extended to Britain by Channon,[5] to France by Dyas,[6] to Italy by Pavan,[7] and to Germany by Thanheiser.[8] Additional studies within the American economy have been performed by Chandler and Salsbury,[9] Newman,[10] and Rumelt.[11]

While most studies in corporate strategy contain an evaluative component, several studies by Hofer,[12] Schoffler, Buzzell, and Heany,[13] Schendel and Patton,[14] and Glueck,[15] have been performed whose major purpose is to investigate the relationship between strategic choice and financial or marketing success. These studies have employed the case studies of firms described in Fortune magazine as sources from which past strategies may be deduced and have evaluated these past strategies by comparing the firm's performance over a set of financial and/or marketing measures. The research has shown a very strong relationship between strategies selected and market and financial successes or failures achieved.

The third area of research into corporate strategy has been that intended to define the information needed by top managers for the formulation of their company's strategies and the means by which managers gather their strategic information. Aguilar,[16] Keegan,[17] Collings,[18] and Wall[19] have all performed studies of this area while Taylor[20] has studied the effects of age and experience on managers' processing of information.

The final area of research, and possibly the most eclectic, is research directed at analysis of the relationship between strategy and the competitive environment. Some of this material is simply anecdotal such as Newman;[21] some behavioral, such as McDonald's[22] analysis of strategic behavior in the context of the game theory pioneered by von Neumann and Morgenstern. Cooper, et al[23] studied the responses of several companies to the introduction of new technology into their industries. The main thrust of the literature, however, has been directed at analysis of the strategic environment and at the generation of procedures for formulating strategies in response to the environment. Generally these tasks are undertaken together, however, the approaches taken range from philosophical approaches to the overall environment such as in Drucker[24,25] and in Ansoff, Declerck, and Hayes[26] to material aimed at analysis of the firm's competitive environment as in Murray,[27] Jauch, Osborn, and Glueck,[28] Cannon,[29] Uyterhoeven, Ackerman, and Rosenblum[30] and Datta.[31] Prescriptive aproaches to strategy formulation range from the organizational approaches of Christensen, Andrews, and Bower,[32] Thompson and Strickland,[33] McNichols,[34] and Uyterhoeven, Ackerman, and Rosenblum[35] to the product and market oriented material of Cannon,[36] Glueck,[37] Argenti,[38] Ansoff,[39] Katz,[40] Porter,[41] Steiner and Miner,[42] and Learned.[43] Of these, the most analytically useful are the works of Ansoff,[44] Katz,[45] Cannon,[46] Steiner and Miner,[47] Porter,[48] and Learned.[49]

These authors' works take two approaches: development of a multidimensional concept of marketing strategy, and extension of the concept.

Cannon defines business strategy as "directional decisions required competitively to accomplish the company's purposes."[50] He rendered this concept operational by analyzing marketing strategy along four dimensions: products, markets (market segments), geographic regions, and distribution-channel characteristics. Learned[51] defined the essential elements of corporate strategy as product (defined in functional terms), market (market segment), price, and distribution channels. Two weaknesses are readily apparent in these lists. First, no consideration is given to a promotion dimension. Thus the effects of advertising efforts are omitted from their analytical models. Second, no explicit connection is made between product design or product differentiation and market segmentation.

Contemporary with these works, Ansoff defined strategy as the "common thread" which extends throughout a business, reflecting the firm's view of itself and its goals. This common thread is made operational through definition of four strategic components: "Product-market scope," "the growth vector," "competitive advantage," and "synergy." "Product-market scope" describes the industries in which the firm competes and specifies the market segments of interest within each industry. The "growth vector" describes the degree to which the firm is increasing or decreasing its involvement in each of its product-markets. "Competitive advantages" are those "particular properties of individual product-markets" in which the firm is superior to its competitors. Finally, "synergy" denotes the joint effects resulting from the sum of the firm's competitive efforts in each of its product-markets. Thus Ansoff defines the firm's relationship to its environment in terms of "product-market scope," "the growth vector," and "competitive advantage," while defining "synergy" as the internal effects resulting from the interaction among the firm's efforts in each product-market.[52]

Composites of this earlier work have appeared recently in Steiner and Miner[53] and in Porter.[54] Steiner and Miner describe marketing strategy along the dimensions of: purpose of the item in terms of user benefits, product scope, applications of products, geographical considerations, distribution channels, and customer set. Porter was more sparing in his list including: pricing policy, type of product, channels, means of differentiation, and diversification or acquisition policies.

The most extensively developed structure for strategic analysis is provided by Katz.[55] In Katz's framework a strategic posture may be identified, described, and evaluated through the study of three component elements: "scope" of a company's endeavors defines the company's view of its own competence and hence its presumed competitive advantage. Katz defines "scope" as consisting of three dimensions:

1. The markets and customers served and their importance to the firm.
2. The types, models, and characteristics of products and the relative sales mix among these offerings.
3. The basis upon which the company chooses to compete, e.g., price, quality or service.

The firm's "scope" will be reflected in its "deployments." "Deployments" are defined by Katz as the relative allocation of resources such as money, production, and management attention among the firm's activities. Finally, Katz defines "specifications" as "measurable parameters which specify important performance characteristics." In his framework, these measurable quantities are used for both description and evaluation, i.e., as both input and output variables depending on the context in which they are used.

Three concepts are evident in Katz' framework. First, the firm's product/market scope is defined by the characteristics of the firm's products and the customers to whom it sells them. Implicitly, product/market scope also defines the set of the firm's competition. Chapter three defines the product/market scope of each of the Japanese and German automanufacturers marketing in the United States in terms of their products and, therefore, their competitors. Second, Katz defines a firm's deployments as its allocation of resources among its activities. In the United States, the Japanese and German firms' activities are essentially those of marketing. Therefore, the deployments reviewed in chapter five are those representing the commitment of resources to competitive effort along the strategic dimensions of marketing: price, product, promotion, and distribution. These deployments are measured by applying Katz' third concept, that of specifications. These "measurable parameters" are employed as indicators of resource deployment along each strategic axis. Thus product effort is measured by the number of models offered by the firm and by the number of product/markets encompassed within the firm's product/market scope. Promotion effort is gauged by the estimated number of dollars spent on annual advertising. Price is measured by the base price of the firm's best selling model. Finally, distribution effort is indicated by the number of dealers retailing the firm's products.

This study incorporates one final extension of strategic analysis, that of the existence of "strategic groups." Porter, expanding on earlier work by Hunt[56] and Newman,[57] stated that,

> Common observation suggests that the firms in an industry often differ from one another in their degree of vertical integration or diversification, the extent to which they advertise and brand their product, whether or not they use captive or exclusive distribution channels, whether they are full-line or narrow-line sellers, whether they operate in the national market or only regionally, whether they are multinational in operation, and so forth. That is, strategies differ among firms in an industry. An industry thus may consist of groups of firms, each group composed of firms that have similar strategies. We define such groups as strategic groups.[58]

The search element of Chapter VIII investigates the possibility of strategic groups among the German and Japanese automanufacturers.

MULTINATIONAL MANAGEMENT

The previous section explored corporate strategy as a theoretical concept, focusing on the application of Katz' analytical framework to the German and Japanese automanufacturers. These firms are not simply domestic companies competing in their own home markets; rather, they are multinational firms penetrating the American market. This section examines the literature and special challenges of multinational management, especially as it relates to strategic issues involved in penetration of a market by foreign firms.

In the literature of multinational management most authors have conentrated on examination of the issues of organization, joint venture, diversification, and international finance. This has resulted in a rather sparse literary treatment of marketing strategy in an international context. However, three areas of international marketing bearing on strategy have appeared. These are the initial penetration decision, product design or the product/market decision, and the choice of an entry strategy.

The initial decision to enter a national market has been discussed by Kolde,[59] Robinson,[60] Schwendiman,[61] and Steiner and Cannon.[62] Kolde's[63] concern was that since a company's success in the market "depends ultimately on the relative degree of correspondence between the qualities of the company product and the requirements of the market," the market-oriented domestic company is preoccupied by its product development, distribution channels, pricing and sales promotion. However, Kolde points out, the decision to market multinationally must consider cross-cultural discontinuities in its environmental variables which may render the firm's domestic plan valueless in an international context. Robinson[64] highlighted the tendency of companies becoming multinationals to transplant their successful domestic strategies to the new market without first considering that the strategies may be suboptimal in a new, and presumably different, environment. Moreover, the corporation's "time dimension in thinking" may well have to be reassessed in the new context due to the longer payoff period associated with international growth and restrictions on monetary movement. Risk as a consideration in multinational expansion was treated by Schwendiman.[65] The top managers of multinationals surveyed in his study recognized two types of risk, political and business. According to Schwendiman, top managers are far too concerned with political risks while neglecting consideration of business risks inherent in foreign operations. Thus overconcern with political risk may cause a parent to starve its subsidiary for capital or materials or may cause the company to seek return of investment so quickly that the firm appears rapacious and exploitative to its host government — nurturing the very political risk which the firm sought to avoid. Schwendiman's prescription (echoing his mentor, R.D. Robinson) is that the firm must recognize that it is operating in an international context and must therefore minimize its risk through flexibility in its approach to foreign ventures. Differing strategies and differing organizational forms may fit different countries and the firm must be willing to adapt itself to the environments prevailing in its host countries. Steiner and Cannon[66] in their treatise on planning in multinational corporations raised one final international issue, that of the well-established relationship between strategy and structure. Steiner and Cannon note that "many subsidiaries of large multinational companies enjoy a high autonomy in planning, often going so far as to determine their own objectives." This local input coupled with the autonomy provided by national requirement or corporate policy choice provides multinational firms with a strong impetus to tailor their strategies to fit local environmental conditions subject to the firm's global design.

The product design decision appears in works by Drucker,[67] Buzzell,[68] and Sorenson and Wichmann.[69] Drucker[70] ascribes the "explosive upsurge of the multinational corporation" to the development of a common world market which transcends national, cultural, and ideological boundaries. This market, engendered by worldwide increases in income and, in particular, in information, is based on a set of common worldwide demands and expectations. The import of this for corporate strategy is that cultural barriers to international competition have fallen. Consequently, a product, or a strategy in general, which has proven successful in one country may well prove successful in another country having a similar level of information available to its consumers. Recognition of common worldwide demands has stimulated research in the areas of product standardization and standardization of marketing methods. Buzzell[71] found that while products often require some degree of modification to fit local conditions, many basic designs are transferrable across national frontiers. Moreover, economies of scale achieved in production of standardized products and the greater ability to spread research and development costs over significantly higher volumes of production offer compelling reasons for companies marketing internationally to attempt standardization of their products. Sorenson and Wichmann[72] surveyed senior executives of multinational corporations marketing consumer products in the United States and Europe and found that whole marketing campaigns could be transferred successfully to foreign markets.   Language, of course, had to be translated and occasionally other cultural modifications were needed, but the overall view of the executives surveyed was that basic themes which were successful in one country tended to be well receivd in other countries.

The final area of multinational literature bearing on marketing strategy is that which discusses the problem of choosing an entry strategy. Authors in this area include: Kolde,[73] Brooke and Remmers,[74] Robock and Simmonds,[75] and Robinson.[76] Kolde, and Brooke and Remmers are concerned about the reasons which may impel a firm to attempt penetration of a foreign market. Kolde considers the marketing factors which may draw a firm to a particular market and influence its penetration strategy. In this, he defines four "strategic criteria" which draw firms to foreign markets and influence their penetration strategies.

1. Preferential treatment. Various spheres of economic influence grew up during and after the colonial era. Firms penetrating markets within their own nation's sphere could rely on governmental assistance and protection from foreign competition resulting in their enjoying local monopoly power. Strategy, therefore, focused on the maintenance and exploitation of this monopoly.

2. The safety valve. An opportunistic criterion, the safety valve involves dumping excess production in a market which would not normally purchase the firm's product. The strategy of penetration was therefore to price the product so low that a market-clearing volume could quickly be achieved, after which the firm would abandon the market in favor of its usual markets.

3. Similitude. The principle of expansion into a country very similar to the firm's home market. A firm may be drawn to attempt penetration of a similar country by the expectation that it can extend its current strategy to new product/markets corresponding to its familiar domestic product/markets.

4. International market research. Kolde defines this criterion as a product of three factors: population, purchasing power, and propensity to buy. This might be termed a searching criterion appealing to firms willing to deviate from their accustomed strategies and to penetrate markets based on a criterion of opportunity rather on a criterion of supposed formal advantage. However, there are risks for, as Kolde points out,

. . . literature on domestic market research often fails to emphasize the significance of this triangular relationship. It does this presumably under the dual assumption that (a) the variance in the population regarding P_2 and P_3 (purchasing power and propensity to buy) is relatively small as far as any particular product is concerned, and (b) pre-existing information can supply the P_2 and P_3 (purchasing power and propensity to buy) necessary to complement any particular set of population data.

In short, let the strategist beware.

Brooke and Remmers,[77] however, take an approach which is not market opportunity oriented, but rather resource oriented. They hold, in contrast to the market pull approach of Kolde, that the push of excess resources and talent often leads a firm into foreign expansion. Their research revealed that, among the firms following "aggressive strategies" who considered their resources underemployed, the greatest impetus was a conviction of the firm's technical superiority, coupled with a wish to spread the costs of research. This superiority may be grounded on a base of product, manufacturing, or management expertise. However, the key factor is the firm's belief that it can best the indigenous competitors in their own home market. This posture, of course, embodies the danger that local reactions to the firm's theoretical superiority may have been estimated incorrectly.

Robock and Simmonds[78] address the question of how a firm may proceed in actually penetrating a chosen market. They see five entry strategies available to the firm subject to the effects of two corporate desires acting as both goals and constraints. The strategies are licensing, export, local warehousing with direct sales staff, local packaging and/or assembly, and full scale local production and marketing. In the context of these alternatives, the firm must weigh in its decision both the company's desire for or aversion to infusion of resources from its home country and also the firm's desire for a certain programmed timing in its investments and returns from the venture.

In contrast to Robock and Simmonds' concentration on the problem of injecting the product into a foreign market, Robinson[79] considers the full scope of the foreign marketing strategy encompassing "the time horizon of management, product quality, design, specialization of product, price, access to channels, and availability of funds for investment in promotion." Robinson follows his prescriptions with a series of cautionary remarks which follow two basic themes. First, are the company's assumptions about the market to be penetrated valid? Second, is the company's proposed penetration strategy, and particularly the product/market component of its strategy, the optimal feasible approach to the markets of this particular nation?

STRATEGY AND MARKETING

The previous section explored the literature of multinational management in three areas related to marketing strategy: initial penetration decisions, product design and product/market decision, and the choice of an entry strategy. The result of these decisions is a level of economic success or failure. Therefore, this section discusses marketing strategies and their impact on corporate profitability.

Marketing-oriented literature treats three areas of direct assistance in understanding and evaluating the strategies employed by the German and Japanese automakers in penetrating the American market. These are: product/market strategies, the effect of market share upon profitability, and strategies of maintaining or enhancing corporate performance through concentration of effort on high market share products.

The choice of product to be employed in a company's penetration is one of its most basic strategic decisions. Biggadike[80] and Day[81] have discussed the profit implications of entering new markets while Miracle and Albaum,[82] Keegan,[83] Brooke and Remmers,[84] Robinson,[85,86] Robock and Simmonds,[87] Schwendiman,[88] and Steiner and Cannon[89] have treated the problems of introducing a product into a foreign market. Two general principles have emerged from this research. First, if a new product is being developed, the firm must attempt to maintain the strongest possible common thread (Ansoff)[90] between its current products and processes and the new product. Second, when a new country is entered, the entrant must be extremely alert to cross-cultural discontinuities (Kolde)[91] which might cripple the firm's marketing abilities. (A relevant example of this is the Japanese home-market fondness for naming their automobiles after flowers; a practice which might well have serious ramifications in the American market.) Finally, Lanzillotti[92] has considered product and product-line strategy as a weapon. In his view, a company may, on occasion, justifiably defend its market position by actually introducing "self competing products" in order to "fence-in" the market. Levitt[93] and Klaw[94] have even shown through example that modern competition has proceeded beyond consideration of the actual physical attributes of the product to forms of "non-generic" competition such as provision of accessory products, financing, and even reference group identification. Each of these features is just as much a part of the product as any physical attribute.

The second area of strategic concern in marketing is that of the relationship between a firm's position in the market and its profitability. A substantial body of empirically oriented literature supports the existence of a strong relationship between a corporation's market share and its return on invested capital. Results of the Profit Impact of Marketing Strategy (PIMS) project have been reported in Schoeffler, Buzzell, and Heany,[95] Gale,[96] and Buzzell, Gale, and Sultan[97] while the staff of the Boston Consulting Group has performed an additional extensive study.[98] While these studies were performed for different purposes, PIMS to seek correlations between market variables and profitability and the Boston Consulting Group to study the effects of volume on cost, they have arrived at remarkably similar results with respect to the effect of market share on corporate profit. Almost universally, both across companies and across industries, profit rises in direct proportion to increase in market share.

Several reasons have been advanced for this relationship. Schoeffler, Buzzell and Heany[99] stated,

> . . . our findings suggest that businesses with relatively large market shares tend to have above average rates of investment turnover, particularly working capital. Also the ratio of marketing expense to sales is generally lower for high-share businesses than for those with small market shares. These differences are indications of economies of scale that may go along with strong market positions.

Buzzell, Gale and Sultan[100] later attempted to explain the relationship more fully in terms of economies of scale, market power, and quality of management. Their analysis of economics of scale showed that "as market share rises, turnover on investment rises only somewhat, but profit margin on sales increases sharply." The PIMS data revealed, rather, that the purchases-to-sales ratio in relation to market share made the largest single difference in corporate costs. Buzzell et al explained this as a combination of increased vertical integration with larger share and the enhanced ability of large volume purchasers to hold down the prices of their suppliers. Additionally they found that large share companies enjoyed a slightly lower ratio of marketing costs to sales and a vastly lower ratio of research and development costs to sales than did small share companies. Each of these factors appears to be readily explained by the presence of true economies of scale, particularly the greater ability to spread fixed costs. Two further findings of special application to the companies studied here were that the effect of market share on profitability was more pronounced when the products were infrequently purchased and when the customers were fragmented rather than concentrated. The automotive industry clearly fits both of these criteria.

The work of the Boston Consulting Group[101] asserts that there exists an overall relationship between corporate volume and costs transcending the recognized existence of learning curves in specific areas of the business. BCG terms this phenomenon the "experience curve." Essentially, as volume rises, the performance of the business as a whole improves. The total business learns to perform. This, of course, implies that the firm's profitability will rise with volume, a fact borne out by the findings of the PIMS project.

In addition to research directed at the overall relationship between market share and profitability, four studies have considered strategic implications of the automotive industry's cost dynamics. Menge[102] investigated the effect of yearly styling changes on the cost structures of U.S. auto producers at various levels of volume. He found that a major effect of yearly model changes was to raise each firm's break-even point by increasing the yearly fixed investment in tooling. However, high volume firms would, at the yearly model change, be discarding tools which had been largely worn out by extensive usage, while low volume firms would be discarding tools long before the end of their useful life. Within this one-year fixed life, therefore, the low volume firms would seldom be able to spread the cost of their tools over the same total number of units as the high volume firms and would be forced to operate from an inherently higher cost position. McGee[103] extended this logic to autobodies while White[104] investigated the overall economics of the U.S. automanufacturers and Rhys[105] compared the production techniques of the European and U.S. auto companies.

Japanese recognition of these compelling economics and their resulting actions have been reported by Abegglen[106,107] and Rose.[108] Abegglen, writing for the Boston Consulting Group, showed that volume affected the profitability of Japanese firms in the same manner as American firms.[109] Japanese penetration efforts in the United States appear to reflect knowledge of this. Their companies have routinely followed strategies of penetration pricing[110] and marginal pricing.[111] Chapter IX contains study of this phenomenon in the specific case of the Japanese automanufacturers.

The establishment of a relationship between market share and profitability has nurtured a literature discussing the strategic implications of this discovery. Day[112] and Biggadike[113] consider the case of entry into new product/markets. Day[114] studied corporations in terms of their current market shares, the position of current products in their life cycles, and the value of their current market shares and determined that, "at the broad level of a new product development strategy, the basic issues are the growth vector, or the direction the firm is moving within the chosen product/market scope, and the emphasis on innovation versus initiation." In his extensive study of new-market entry, Biggadike[115] found that entry into new markets was often a highly unprofitable business. He studied a group of firms who, after entry, managed to remain in the market and still fifty-nine per cent of his sample failed to achieve their market share objectives. This occurred even though most of the firms in his sample had set very low initial objectives, wherein even achievement of these objectives did not foreordain profitability. Biggadike reported, moreover, that in his opinion, "in large part . . . their poor performance was self-inflicted. In effect, these entrants obtained the market share they deserved and this, in turn, contributed to their poor financial performance." His prescriptions for successful entry were two. First, "entry on a large scale is necessary for eventual success in rapid growth markets." He found that unaggressive entry in the presence of strong competitors resulted in the vitiation of any sales gains produced by penetration. Market share could not be achieved without large scale entry. Second, "managers should evaluate entrant businesses on the basis of relative share achieved and capitalized ROI." Short-term performance is generally damaged by expenditures to achieve a strong position in the product/market. Managers must be aware of this and accept it as the price of future success in the market. (The findings in Chapter IX support Biggadike's findings.)

The final area of research is that relating to the maintenance and enhancement of corporate performance. Authors have taken three viewpoints in analyzing this area: resource allocation among the company's product/markets, analysis of strategies aimed at adjusting market share, and analysis of the limitations of volume-oriented strategies.

Catry and Chevalier,[116] Wind and Claycamp,[117] and Day[118] have all considered the resource allocation decision. Catry and Chevalier[119] proposed that the decision for future marketing investment in any product/market should be evaluated along three dimensions: the product's position in its life cycle, the firm's current share of the product/market, and the firm's desire for share in the product/market. Wind and Claycamp[120] accepted these basic propositions, but argued that earlier research did not provide "a comprehensive approach for product line planning based on all three measures — sales, market share, and profitability which are integrally tied to positioning the product by market segment." Wind and Claycamp attempted to construct a planning procedure using a "product evaluation matrix." This matrix, composed of the products' definitions, their key markets, and their current sales, market shares, and profitability would then be used to test various possible allocations of the firm's marketing resources. Thus, product/market strategy and the overall marketing strategy could be determined to seek maximum long-term gain. Day[121] proposed that the company's products be divided into four classes employing a taxonomy based on sales growth and market share. He styled the low growth/dominant share products "cash cows," the high growth/dominant share products "stars," the low growth/subordinate share products "dogs," and the high growth/subordinate share products "problem children." Division into these classes facilitated examination of each product's strategic implications. Cash cows are the firm's basic strength. They throw off the cash that makes other products possible. Therefore, Day recommends that the firm place its top resource priority on maintaining the market share of these products. On the other hand, Day cautions that "pressure to overinvest through product proliferation and market expansion should be resisted unless prospects for expanding primary demands are unusually attractive." Stars represent the future. They are the products which are currently heavy cash consumers due to their high rate of growth, but whose dominant position in their markets gives promise of future high rates of profit and cash inflow. These products also enjoy a high priority for corporate resources to maintain or expand their already substantial market shares. Additionally, Day proposes that "particular attention must be given to obtaining a large share of the new users or new applications that are the source of growth in the market." Dogs are marginally profitable at best; their low market shares generally place them at a cost disadvantage. Consequently, as long as competition remains strong, any resources committed to a dog are essentially lost. This leaves four strategic alternatives open to the firm: a niche strategy in which efforts are focused on domination of a defensible segment, a harvesting strategy in which the dog's cash flow is quickly drawn off, a divestment strategy under which the dog is sold, and an abandonment strategy in which the dog is simply dropped from the product line. Problem children are the firm's troublesome products. These are high growth and, therefore, high cash demand situations in which the firm has not gained a dominant market position. Since lack of market share foreshadows lack of future profitability, the firm has two alternatives: commit sufficient resources to turn the product into a star or treat the problem child as a dog and follow one of the restrictive strategies appropriate to that class of products. Overall, Day's approach to product portfolio strategy hinges on cash flow planning. Cash cows and the liquidation of dogs and problem children provide the corporate lifeblood which is directed to maintain the cash cows, nurture stars and strengthen problem children, in that priority. The degree to which a firm may attempt to reform promising problem children is constrained by the cash flow remaining after higher priority needs have been filled. Therefore, Day's approach determines not only the firm's product portfolio, but also its willingness to participate in product/markets in which it is weak, such as in new or unaccustomed product/markets.

Day's recommendations are based on the earlier work of Buzzell, Gale and Sultan[122] and Bloom and Kotler[123] who studied overall product/market strategy. Buzzell, Gale and Sultan found three major strategic forms: building strategies, holding strategies, and harvesting strategies. They noted that "in many cases, even a marginally acceptable rate of return can be earned only by attaining some minimum level of market share." Hence, companies below this level have two alternatives: build share, or liquidate it. Share building was found to be a slow process which depressed short-term financial results. However, it is generally the price of eventual profitability. Holding strategies were found to be by far the most common strategic choice among established firms. Resource demands of holding strategies are less stringent than for share building. However, Buzzell et al. found it hard to draw generalizations for profit maximizing holding strategies. The variance in competitive conditions was simply too great. Higher return on investment was, however, associated with those higher share firms charging premium prices for what were generally higher quality goods. They also found "ROI is usually greater for large share businesses when they spend more than their major competitors, in relation to sales, on sales force effort, advertising and promotion, and research and development." Evidently, large share firms improved their financial returns by employing strategies of quality, promotion, and distribution rather than by emphasizing price competition. Not surprisingly, the interests of small volume firms were found to lie in the opposite direction. The researchers found that "on the average, ROI is highest for these businesses when their prices are somewhat below the average of leading competitors and when their rates of spending on marketing and R&D are relatively low." The opposite of a share building strategy is a harvesting strategy. This alternative was investigated by Talley[124] and by Kotler[125] and is summarized by Buzzell, Gale and Sultan[126] as a strategy of necessity rather than a strategy of choice. A harvesting strategy entails the liquidation of market share to improve short-term profits or cash flows. Effectively, management harvests the fruits of its past investments in share building. Buzzell et al. see this as a strategy generally precipitated by necessity, however; lowered market share will result in lowered future profitability, a result generally regarded as undesirable.

Bloom and Kotler[127] discussed methods of implementing four strategies for companies enjoying high market shares: share building, share maintenance, share reduction, and risk reduction. When companies conclude their market position to be suboptimal, Bloom and Kotler see four methods of implementing a share building strategy. The most effective, in their opinion, is product innovation. Unfortunately, it is also the most risk laden. Three safer strategies are market segmentation, distribution innovation, and promotional innovation. While these are basically safer, however, they are not risk free. Bloom and Kotler caution that the firm must carefully plan its innovation and lead from basic strength. Otherwise, the company may end up disastrously advertising its weaknesses. When a company concludes that its market share is optimal, or at least at the desired level, a strategy of share maintenance is appropriate. Bloom and Kotler hold with Franklin's dictum that "The best defense is a fisty offense." They recommend that the best procedure for maintaining market share is for the firm to act like a firm which is trying to build market share. That is: product, customer, distribution, and promotional innovation coupled with redoubled efforts at efficient operation. Failing this, their second proposal is that the firm fortify its market. This involves introduction of products to "plug holes in the market" forestalling competitive entries. As Bloom and Kotler note, this is the multibrand strategy so popular in consumer products (and recognized very early by Lanzillotti).[128] Their final defense rests on a confrontation strategy. In this case, the dominant firm defends its share through extensive price cutting and promotional campaigns directed upon interlopers. Besides the expense, this type of defense opens the firm to legal and other risks. Therefore, Bloom and Kotler do not recommend its use. Their third strategic alternative is that of share reduction. At times, high market share may be a legal, political, or social embarrassment. Alternatively, the firm's customer base may include far too many marginal customers. In these cases, Bloom and Kotler recommend the adoption of a less competitive strategy. Prices may be raised, promotion and distribution reduced in order to raise immediate profit and lower market share to less dominant levels. A final strategy for high volume companies is that of risk reduction. This included any behavior which a corporation adopts to lessen the level of risk it bears due to its high share. Implementation may include: public relations efforts, gentle treatment of competitors (competitive pacification), encouraging the government to rely on the company as a supplier (dependency), legislation, diversification, and social concern (social responsiveness).

The final strategic consideration in marketing is that of limits which may exist in pursuit of efficiency and market share. Abernathy and Wayne[129] have found apparently inherent limits in real-world learning curves due to the flexibility in product necessary to reach high volume in many markets. This flexibility requirement limits the cost reductive effect of increasing volume. In contrast to this, however, are the findings of the Boston Consulting Group which found that firms continually improved their performance as they gained experience. Thus, the question of possible limits on experience remains open.

The question of limits on market share has been addressed by Fruhan.[130] He did not question the value of market share, but rather cautioned that concentration on market share may be disastrous to the firm if the firm is somehow prevented from gaining a larger share after committing its resources to the quest. Fruhan posed three questions which a company should ask before committing itself to a pursuit of market share:

1. "Does the company have the financial resources necessary to win – and then support – the level of sales implied by its market share target; or, if it does not have these resources, can it acquire them at acceptable cost?"

2. "Will the company find itself in a viable position if its drive for an expanded market share should be thwarted – by antitrust action, say – before it had reached its market share target?"

3. "Will regulatory authorities permit the company to achieve its objective with the strategy it has chosen to follow?"

The strongest cautionary notes of all, however, come from two early authors in the field, Tilles[131] in 1963, and Levitt[132] in 1960. Tilles reminded his readers that many companies have been profitable in one size and utterly unprofitable in a larger size. While more recent research has established the pivotal role of market share in profitability, Tilles' caution that a company must not lose sight of its own competences still stands. Singleminded pursuit of growth may be just as destructive to the firm as neglect of its market position. As Bloom and Kotler[133] and Fruhan[134] have shown, large market share is no shield against overextension or outright mismanagement.

A final insight echoes from Levitt's early paper.[135] Viewing the contemporary scene in 1960, he cautioned companies to be very careful in defining their markets. Expending a corporation's resources to achieve the dominant position in a market which is in reality only a part of a much wider market could easily result in the firm becoming strategically trapped, holding only a small share of the larger market and bereft of the resources necessary to alter its position.

APPLICATION

This study in corporate strategy analyzes the marketing strategies employed by multinational companies in penetrating the American market. Its basic structure is that of a study in corporate strategy. The issues addressed are multi-dimensional, spanning product, price, advertising, and distribution behavior. Changes in each firm's position along each strategic dimension are included in the analysis together with analysis of changes in each firm's product/market scope over time. The extent of strategic analysis is limited, however, by the nature of the firms included in the study. During the period analyzed, none of the firms manufactured automobiles in the United States. Their American activities were restricted to marketing efforts. Therefore, only the dimensions of marketing strategy are included in this study.

Concentration on marketing strategy requires the study to address three analytical issues. First, analysis of each firm's strategic development in terms of its overall competitive behavior along the strategic dimensions of product/market scope, advertising, pricing, and distribution must be performed. This is the subject of Chapter III. Second, the two national groups included in the study must be analyzed to describe their competitive behavior in adapting marketing strategies to the American market and to determine whether the two nationalities followed different strategic paths. Analyses of the firms' and groups of firms' strategies are reported in Chapters IV through VIII. Third, the degree of relative success achieved by each firm in the American market must be evaluated. This is the subject of Chapter IX.

The study, therefore, flows from the description of corporate strategies performed in Chapter III through the strategic analyses of Chapters IV to VIII ending in the evaluation of strategic success reported in Chapter IX.

III

Product/Market Segmentation Among German and Japanese Automotive Importers

Strategic theory defines in general terms the concepts of product/market scope, resource deployment, and specifications. In order to proceed with this study, it is necessary to apply these concepts specifically to the industry and firms to be analyzed. Doing this means specifying the firms to be studied, the time period over which they are to be studied, and the various dimensions along which the firms' strategies are to be evaluated.

This chapter specifies the firms and time period selected for study and the reasons for their selection. The variables used in strategic analysis are defined and the source of data for each is described. The variables are then associated into sets of vectors, summarized in Figure 3-1, describing each firm's marketing strategy. A methodology for specification of each firm's product/market scope is then described and applied. This results in two sets of findings: those describing evolution of the German and Japanese automakers' overall product/market scope, and those describing the evolution of each firm's individual product/market scope and the product/market strategy underlying its product/market scope.

SELECTION OF FIRMS FOR STUDY

The Japanese and German firms collectively dominated the American market for imported automobiles between 1965 and 1976. As Figure 1-1 illustrated, their market share never fell below 72% during the decade and rose to 85% by 1976. During that period the British firms' total share declined from 10% to 4.3% while those of the next strongest competitor, Italy, never exceeded their unusually high 1975 share of 6.7%. The recent history of import penetration of the American market is primarily a history of German and Japanese competition; other nation's firms never maintained more than a marginal position in the market. Therefore, analysis was focused on these two groups of dedicated competitors, and excluded nations whose firms have not maintained a strong presence in the American market.

This is, consequently, a study of the strategic decisions taken by top managers of German and Japanese auto manufacturers under conditions of increasing competition among themselves in penetrating the American market. Both the firms and the time period to be studied were selected to meet these requirements.

This study included only firms based and owned in Japan or West Germany that offer one or more passenger automobiles for sale in the United States. The study includes only those market segments in which one or more Japanese or German auto manufacturers participate. Firms meeting these criteria are:

1. Toyota
2. Nissan (Datsun)
3. Toyo-Kogyo (Mazda)
4. Honda
5. Subaru
6. Bayerische Motoren Werke (BMW)
7. Daimler-Benz (Mercedes)
8. Volkswagen (division of Volkswagenwerk)
9. Porsche-Audi (division of Volkswagenwerk)

Restriction of the study to these firms serves three purposes:

1. The U.S. market for imported automobiles is essentially a Japanese and German one. Thus, the study includes each firm's major import competitors.
2. Restriction of the study to Japanese and German firms excludes fringe and transient competitors who are neither purposeful nor dedicated to penetration of the American market.
3. Since a basic purpose of the study is to analyze the competitive behavior of firms whose goals and strategies have been determined in foreign countries, the study excluded all foreign firms owned or substantially controlled by companies based in the United States on the grounds that their goals and strategies are set for them by United States firms.

TIME PERIOD

The study covers the years 1966 to 1976 inclusive. This period was chosen for two reasons:

1. During this period the Japanese manufacturers entered the U.S. market in strength and encountered an entrenched German

presence. The differing initial market position of the two national groups will, therefore, allow comparison of their strategic behavior resulting from their differing starting positions.

2. Extending the analysis backward beyond the mid-60's would result in the inclusion of years in which there was either no direct competition or solely American competition with German firms. These relatively uncompetitive years conflict with the overall purpose of the study which is to study foreign corporate behavior under conditions of foreign competition for a domestic market.

Two exceptions are made to this time specification. First, if a given firm's competitive behavior appears to reflect the influence of events which occurred prior to 1966, analysis of that firm's behavior is extended to include those earlier years necessary to understanding of the firm's later behavior. Second, if a firm entered the American market after 1966, analysis of its competitive behavior commences in the year of the firm's entry.

STRATEGIC DIMENSIONS

Description of a firm's marketing strategy requires measurement of the firm's position along each of four dimensions: price, promotion, distribution, and product. Measurement, in this study, is performed by a set of numeric control variables whose individual values describe the firm's position along each dimension. Collectively, these control variables describe the firm's strategic posture in each year.

The distribution dimension is measured by a variable representing the total number of U.S. dealers carrying the firm's products at year end.

The promotion dimension is measured by a variable representing the estimated yearly total number of dollars spent within the U.S. by a firm to advertise its products. The value of this variable included spending on network and spot television, network and spot radio, billboards, and magazines.

Price is measured by two variables whose usage is determined by analytical purpose. For purpose of product/market definition, price is measured by a set of variables whose values are the list prices of the firm's models at the yearly time of model introduction. For purposes of strategic analysis, price is measured by a variable whose value is the price of the firm's most popular model in that year. The firm's most popular model is that which achieved the highest number of unit sales in the year being described.

The product dimension is measured by a set of variables whose usage, also, is determined by analytical purpose. For purposes of product/market definition, products are described by a set of variables each representing a product attribute. Bulk is measured by the model's unladen weight in pounds. Physical size is measured by the model's wheelbase in inches. Power is measured by the maximum number of brake horsepower generated by the model's standard engine. For purposes of analysis of strategic evolution, the preceding product dimension variables for each year are replaced by two computed variables: the number of models produced in each year, and the number of market segments in which competition was offered.

DATA SOURCES

Values for each control variable for each firm each year were drawn from the following data sources.

Values for the distribution dimension variable are calculated from yearly editions of *Ward's Automotive Yearbook*. Ward's compiles the number of retail outlets, broken down by firm by state for each year. The value of the distribution variable for each year is computed by summing the values in that year for each firm.

Values for the promotion dimension variable are based on estimates of corporate advertising expenditures by Leading National Advertisers, Inc. These estimates have been compared with estimates provided by the Radio Advertising Bureau, Television Bureau of Advertising, and the Outdoor Advertising Bureau and have proven consistent.

Values for the price dimension variables are taken from the introduction prices for each model from each firm as they appeared in the yearly issues of *The Automotive News Almanac*.

Values for the product attribute variables for each model from each firm are taken as they appeared in the "Product Specifications" section in yearly issues of *The Automotive News Almanac*.

DESCRIPTION OF STRATEGIES

As described in the strategic theory section, corporate strategies are multidimensional in scope. Consequently, in this study each firm's strategies are described by a set of vectors whose elements represent the firm's position or direction of movement along a strategic dimension.

The strategic posture vector is a five element vector describing a firm's position along each strategic dimension during one year. The five elements are:

1. The number of models offered for sale in the United States by the firm during the year,
2. The number of product/market groups in which the firm's products competed during the year,
3. The total number of dollars spent on advertising in the United States during the year,
4. The number of dealers retailing the firm's products at the end of the year, and
5. The price of the firm's model achieving the highest level of sales in the United States during the year.

The strategic changes vector is based on the same five dimensions as the strategic posture vector. However, where the strategic posture vector represents a firm's absolute position on each strategic dimension during one year, the strategic changes vector represents the relative change in a firm's position along each strategic dimension between one year and the next. Thus, where the strategic posture vector reveals a firm's strategic position, the strategic changes vector reveals a firm's direction of strategic movement.

The final vector employed in describing each firm's strategy is the strategic evolution vector. This vector also consists of five elements representing the number of models, numbers of product/market groups, number of advertising dollars, number of dealers, and price of most popular model. However, rather than reflecting short-term position or direction, the elements of a firm's strategic evolution vector reflect the average annual change along each dimension during the period covered by the study. The evolution vector thus adds a long-term perspective to the information provided by the posture and changes vectors.

IDENTIFICATION OF PRODUCT/MARKET SCOPES

A firm's product/market scope is defined by the differentiating attributes of its products. The wide diversity of automobiles available in the American market today reflects competitors' strenuous efforts in product differentiation.

This study measures corporate efforts at penetration through product differentiation by comparing each of the firm's products with its other products and with those of its competitors in a cluster analysis. If a firm targeted a model at a gap in the market or constructed a model with a combination of attributes uncommon to pre-existing models, the cluster analysis reveals the presence of a new group of differentiated products. If, however, a firm chose to produce a product whose attributes closely parallelled its other products or those of its competitors, the cluster analysis associates the products in one product/market group. Thus, the extent to which each firm has followed a strategy of product differentiation is reflected in the number of product/market groups in which the firm's products competed in each year.

METHODOLOGY

Frank and Green[1] describe three approaches to construction of proximity clusters: distance measure, correlation measures, and similarity measures. Distance measures may be computed in a number of ways; however, by far the most common method is to compute the Euclidean distance of each object from its cluster centroid. Clusters are then constructed to minimize the within cluster distances. There are two weaknesses in this approach: correlation among the characteristics and non-comparability of measurement scales. The correlation problem may be resolved by performing a principal components analysis of the data prior to clustering. There is, however, the drawback that the resulting components may be difficult to interpret for managerial decisionmaking. The noncomparability problem is generally resolved by standardizing the data before clustering. Correlation measures may be computed through the use of inverse factor analysis. While this approach removes the intercorrelation problem inherent in distance measurement procedures, it is at the cost of a degradation in the quality of information resulting from the analysis. Similarity measures are used in instances where the data are dichotomous or multichotomous. As the data in this study are metric in all cases, the use of a similarity technique would require degradation of the data with a concomitant loss of part of the information available from the data.

Frank, Massey, and Wind[2] define the most meaningful market segmentation scheme as that segmentation which minimizes:

Variance $\qquad \left[\sum_{i \epsilon j} \frac{d f_i}{d x_j} \right] \qquad$ over all $j \epsilon h$

Where: $\dfrac{d f_i}{d x_j}$

is the response of the ith individual included in the jth microsegment. And, all j microsegments are members of the hth macrosegment.

This concept is rendered operational in this study by defining each distinctive automotive model as an individual response by a manufacturer to his perception of the existence of a specific microsegment. Seldom, however, is any one microsegment of sufficient size to support economic production and sale of a model. Thus each model must appeal to a relatively homogenous set of microsegments which are being served by a corresponding set of relatively homogenous (not strongly differentiated) products.

This set of similar, highly substitutable products, therefore, defines the industry's collective perception of the existence of a macrosegment including the markets at which the products of a product/market group are targeted.

This study discovers these macrosegments by performing a cluster analysis utilizing the Howard-Harris algorithm. This procedure clusters stimuli by application of the criterion of minimum within-group variance at each level of clustering.[3] The program procedes iteratively, splitting the group having the greatest within-group variance and reassigning individuals to clusters on the basis of minimum within-group variance. At each iteration the remaining with-group variance and group memberships are recorded.

STOPPING CRITERION

If the market for Japanese and German automobiles consists of a number of definite macrosegments, as hypothesized at the beginning of the study, the remaining within-group variance should drop drastically as the macrosegments are identified. Once the clustering procedure has identified the macrosegments and begins to decompose the relatively homogenous macrosegments into their component microsegments, the additional within-group variance explained by successive iterations should be insignificant. Figure 3-2 illustrates that this is, in fact, the case. Inspection of Figure 3-2, however, does not provide a statistical means of identifying the point at which macrosegment membership has been defined and beyond which spurious segments are being generated. Hartigan[4] provides such a procedure. He argues that while the ratio:

$$R = \left[\frac{eP(M,K)}{eP(M,K+1)} \right]\text{-}1 \qquad (M=K+1)$$

Where:

$M =$	the number of subjects
$K =$	the number of clusters
$P(M,K) =$	the partition of M subjects into K clusters
$e\,P(M,K) =$	the error as measured by the sum of the Euclidean distance of the subjects from the cluster centroid

does not exactly follow an F distribution due to the upward bias resulting from the clustering procedure's attempt to maximally reduce the sum of the within cluster variances with each successive iteration, the distribution is close enough to be operationally useful. While a critical value drawn from a true F distribution would be computed with N and (M-K-1)N degrees of freedom (where N= the number of variables), Hartigan suggests correcting for the upward bias by only increasing the number of clusters when the ratio is easily larger than the critical value. He suggests a ratio of at least ten as a reasonable requirement. Ratios for successive clustering iterations are shown in Figure 3-3.

PRODUCT/MARKET DEVELOPMENT AND COMPETITION AMONG THE GERMAN AND JAPANESE AUTOMANUFACTURERS

Evidence of three competitive changes emerges from data shown in Figure 3-4: the number of models has risen 158%; the number of product/market groups has jumped 11%; and the number of firms competing has climbed from 6 to 9 firms. However, the changes were not concurrent. Moreover, the firms did not choose to follow like competitive paths.

Data on the number of models, number of product/market groups, and number of firms indicates that competition in the market has evolved in six distinct phases. The years 1965 to 1967 saw all six firms, Volkswagen, BMW, Mercedes-Benz, Porsche-Audi, Toyota, and Nissan, add models while remaining in their same basic product markets. Both Honda and Subaru followed the strategy of developing a new product/market group, that of the very small lowpriced minicars. As Day and Shocker[5] would predict, this effort began with Honda's positioning of its first entry right on the edge of Porsche-Audi's weakest line, the NSU. By 1969, Honda and Subaru had each developed a separate product/market for their products. The years 1969 to 1971 were a period of heavy model proliferation without development of new product/market groups. Firms increased the number of models entered in their current groups and entered the groups which other competitors had already developed. While the number of models increased 87%, from 38 to 71, the number of product/market groups declined 23%, from 9 to 7. It was in the 1971 to 1973 period that development of new product/markets became fashionable in the industry. While each firm continued to compete in roughly the same number of product/market groups, and the total number of models offered actually declined, the market was shattered into over twice as many definable product/market groups rising from 7 to 16. Where in 1971 it was not unusual for one group to contain half a dozen competitors, by 1973 no groups held more than three. 1973 to 1975 was another period of consolidation. The firms maintained their number of models. However, the models were repositioned to approach one-fourth fewer product/market groups, dropping from 16 to 12. The data for 1975-1976 indicate that the firms resumed adding models. Moreover, Volkswagen, Porsche-Audi, Toyota and Toyo-Kogyo resumed adding product/market groups.

While analysis of the market as a whole reveals the pronounced changes in grouping of products which have occurred over time, the competitive behavior of firms within the market has differed markedly. Some firms have followed multiproduct/market group strategies; others have confined their efforts to a single product/market. Some have sought product/markets containing little or no competition; others have willingly embraced highly competitive product/markets.

Figure 3-5 shows that Mercedes-Benz, Porsche-Audi, Toyota, and Nissan have followed long-standing multiproduct/market group strategies with Mercedes consistently penetrating 4 to 5 groups while Porsche-Audi generally offered 3 to 4 groups, Toyota centered about 3 and 1/2 and Nissan (since 1970) also averaged about 3 and 1/2. Volkswagen and Toyo-Kogyo have more recently moved in this direction, changing from strategies emphasizing multiple models in a limited number of product/market groups, Volkswagen jumping from 1 to 3 groups and Toyo-Kogyo from 2 to 3. Bayerische Motoren Werke, Honda, and Subaru have consistently restricted their offerings to a very small number of groups, generally one, or at most, two.

Each firm's direct competitors are identified in Figure 3-6. Toyota, Nissan, and Toyo-Kogyo have competed in every year, while Honda and Subaru have never competed with Bayerische Motoren Werke and Mercedes. Volkswagen and Mercedes have also never competed with one another. All of the other pairings reflect intermittent competition. Richer information is provided in Figure 3-7. Mercedes dominance of its product/markets is reflected in its average of less than one competitor in each product/market group, only .72 competitors per group. Porsche-Audi, Honda, and Subaru each faced significant competition in their chosen product/markets at 1.87, 1.78, and 1.88 competitors per group respectively; however, the competition stems from vastly differing sources. Porsche-Audi, with its multiproduct/market group strategy, has faced every other Japanese and German firm. Honda and Subaru, however, offer products only in the small-car groups and consequently have faced a much more restricted set of competitors. Toyota, Nissan, and Toyo-Kogyo, aiming their products at the middle of the market, have all faced comparatively high levels of competition in their product/market groups generally from each other, partially explaining their respective 2.70, 2.63, and 2.8 competitors per product/market group.

INDIVIDUAL PRODUCT/MARKET STRATEGIES
OF EACH OF THE AUTOMANUFACTURERS

The German and Japanese automanufacturers have followed strikingly different product/market strategies in penetrating the American market. This section examines each firm's product/market strategy and highlights the changes implemented during its evolution. Finally, the firm's product/market strategies are compared and contrasted revealing the diversity of their penetration efforts. This diversity is summarized in Figure 3-8.

Volkswagen

The data show that Volkswagen only recently began to participate in different product/markets while reducing the total number of models offered. Volkswagen's success in America was founded on one model, the Type I or Beetle, which like Ford's original Model T, offered a combination of economy and durability that endured over an astounding number of years. Like Ford in the 1920's[6,7,8] Volkswagen became a prisoner of its own success by failing to exploit its early market lead through development of a line of products. Volkswagen offered only two engines throughout the decade of the sixties and did not offer a choice of frame (wheelbase) until 1971. Even with the early 70's extension of its product line, Volkswagen still depended on the Type I for over two-thirds of its unit sales in 1974.

Toyota and Nissan

Toyota and Nissan followed a very different product/market strategy in approaching the American market. Each of these firms entered the United States with several models in place. Moreover, these products were well differentiated. Even in 1965, Toyota offered three different frames and a choice of three engines while Nissan provided four frames and four different engines, one of which had a full six cylinders. Each firm proceeded apace in extending into further product/markets, until by 1976 Toyota offered twelve models on five frames with a choice of four engines, while Nissan marketed ten models on five frames with three different engines. Volkswagen's six models, four frames, and four engines pale by comparison with the varied selection provided by its chief competitors. Moreover, Volkswagen has retained an image as a "one car company" while Toyota and Nissan have become known for providing a variety of products. The parallel with the 1920's confrontation of Ford and General Motors is compelling.[9,10] Like Ford, Volkswagen restricted its product line until its competition had acquired a significant strategic advantage. Toyota and Nissan, however, followed a GM-like strategy of penetrating several product/markets concurrently. As Chapter V demonstrates, Volkswagen committed a grievous error. By the time Volkswagen's management took corrective action, it was a case of too little and too late. Toyota and Nissan had become established in their product/markets and Volkswagen's pre-eminence had been destroyed.

Toyo-Kogyo

Toyo-Kogyo provides a study of the late entrant attempting to emulate the demonstrably successful product/market strategy of its predecessors. The company entered the United States in 1971 with eight models and by 1972 had raised its offerings to twelve models competing in three product/market groups, a level of effort roughly comparable to those of Nissan and Toyota. The company was unable to sustain this performance for a number of reasons, one of which was the low level of fuel economy provided by its rotary engines. However, Toyo-Kogyo has consistently marketed a relatively large number of models and has attempted to rebuild its line to approximately equal the lines of Toyota and Nissan in their extent. Additionally, Toyo-Kogyo has continued to produce both piston and rotary engines for its automobiles and therefore to maintain an appearance of technological innovativeness, while concurrently maintaining the company's monopoly of the market for rotary powered automobiles.

Porsche-Audi

Porsche-Audi offers another example of a firm which has, at times, provided a large number of models participating in a large number of product/market groups. Porsche-Audi, however, did not confine its product offerings to closely related product/market groups in the manner of the other German and Japanese companies, but rather maintained products in several widely divergent groups. The original NSU products, gained in the NSU-Auto Union merger which produced Audi, were unique. They included both the second smallest (1106 lbs.), second most underpowered (36 HP) automobile provided by the German and Japanese automakers since 1965 and also the only rotary powered automobile until Toyo-Kogyo's entry, the double-rotor R0-80. Auto Union provided its middle-class oriented sedans, and Porsche has continued to manufacture its expensive sportscars. This collection has provided Porsche-Audi with what is easily the most diverse line of automobiles among the German and Japanese companies. This has resulted in two basic competitive difficulties for Porsche-Audi. First, there is no common set of features across their products upon which a sales campaign may be based. This has forced Porsche-Audi to promote its lines separately rather than employing the other firm's tactic of promoting their whole product line in most of their advertising materials. Second, Porsche-Audi's diverse products have brought it into competition with all of the other German and Japanese firms. Consequently, a strengthening of any firm's competitive efforts will almost certainly result in some degree of injury to Porsche-Audi. The company, spanning the market as it did, had to face the strategic decision of whether to continue attempting to compete with the entire group of German and Japanese companies, or to follow a retrenchment strategy of concentration on its most popular models. Porsche-Audi's solution was to drop the NSU line entirely and to concentrate its efforts on the Audi and Porsche lines. Thus, Porsche-Audi redefined its product/market scope to exclude lower priced "economy" models and to concentrate on sedans aimed at middle socio-economic levels and on expensive sportscars.

The upward redefinition of both Vokswagen's and Porsche-Audi's product/market scopes represents a shift of their product/market strategies in the direction of two German firms which have always followed high quality, high price product/market strategies: Mercedes and Bayerische Motoren Werke. Appendix B shows, however, that even with their concentration on "better" products the product/market scopes of Volkswagen and Porsche-Audi seldom overlap those of BMW and Mercedes. Moreover, BMW and Mercedes are revealed as generally participating in different product/markets.

Mercedes-Benz

Mercedes participates in the highest priced product/markets among the German and Japanese automakers. Throughout the period of this study, the company followed a strategy of widely diverse products, all of top quality, but extending over many automotive forms including coupes, sedans, roadsters, convertibles, and even a limousine. Further, Mercedes entered the period offering a selection of seven engines, one a diesel, and has consistently provided its customers with an unusually wide number of possible power-trains. Finally, each basic Mercedes model enjoys its own frame, giving the firm easily the widest range of automobile sizes among the German and Japanese producers. There has, however, been a great change in the source of power for these automobiles. Where 1965 saw Mercedes with one diesel powered model, the 190DC, which was simply an underpowered variant of the standard 190C, by 1976 the firm offered two models designed specifically for diesel power, the 240D and 300D. These models have turned what was once an exotic sideline into the mainstay of Mercedes' effort in the United States, capturing 94% of Mercedes' American sales in 1976. Thus, the firm's U.S. sales now depend very heavily on a related pair of product/markets which barely existed in 1965.

Bayerische Motoren Werke

Bayerische Motoren Werke entered the American market far later than Mercedes, but with a comparable product/market strategy of consistently offering higher quality, higher price products. BMW, however, has also been consistent in maintaining a product/market scope which is distinctly different from that maintained by Mercedes-Benz. Direct comparison reveals that BMW has always attempted penetration of far fewer product/markets than has Mercedes. In general, moreover, BMW'S products offer a higher power to weight ratio, a shorter wheelbase, and much less weight than Mercedes' products. In short, BMW has evidently designed its products for penetration of a more performance-oriented and less luxury-oriented set of product/markets than has Mercedes. This basic divergence in product/market strategy has been recently reinforced by Mercedes' introduction of its 450 series of automobiles, a series offering power to weight ratios 14% lower than those of the top-of the-line BMW 3.0SI, with 18% more weight, significantly longer wheelbases (except for the 450SL) and prices around 50% higher than that of the BMW 3.0SI.

Honda and Subaru

The product/market strategies employed by Honda and Subaru in penetrating the American market stand in sharp contrast to those of Bayerische Motoren Werke and Mercedes-Benz. Where the preceding two firms concentrated on product/markets at the top of those penetrated by the German and Japanese automakers, Honda and Subaru aimed at the bottom.

Honda has been unique among the German and Japanese firms in following what until recently was a one product strategy. Honda's product line consisted entirely of its Civic, a low-powered low-priced vehicle providing basic transportation. Gradually variants of the Civic were introduced, based on Honda's technological innovation, the stratified charge engine, and finally a completely new model, the Accord, was introduced late in the 1976 model year. Honda's success, however, has remained dependent on the basic transportation end of the market. The firm offers a minimal number of options on its products and has only recently produced an easily shifted transmission, the Hondamatic, with which the firm has attempted penetration of product/markets which demand automatic transmissions.

Subaru entered the market in 1969 with the Subaru 360, an automobile so small (70.9 inch wheelbase), so light (886 pounds) and so poorly powered (25 horsepower), that much of the industry did not seriously consider it an automobile. The market ratified this judgment with sales figures too low to be tabulated in the industry's trade journals. In 1970, however, Subaru introduced the first of its "star" line. These automobiles conformed to the approximate length of the smaller Datsuns, Toyotas, and Mazdas, but at lower weights and levels of horsepower. They also, however, were offered at lower prices than the other Japanese and German offerings and did manage to achieve a low level of market acceptance. From 1971-1975, Subaru gradually expanded its model offerings. However, all of these models were based on a single frame and a single engine. Therefore, Subaru was attempting penetration of the Amrican market employing essentially the same product strategy which was proving so destructive to Volkswagen. Chapter IX documents the cost of this. By 1976 Subaru had altered its product/market strategy slightly to encompass two basic thrusts. First, the company extended its lines of small, very light, low-powered automobiles offered at low prices. Evidently, in this the company is attempting to capture markets for products which offer features beyond those provided by Honda's narrow product offerings and yet not at the level (and price) of the products offered by Nissan and Toyota. Second, the company has developed a niche for a very highly differentiated product, the light, inexpensive, four-wheel-drive wagon. Other producers have made occasional competitive advances toward this product/market, such as the two-wheel-drive Honda Civic wagon. However, most station wagons are both large and expensive while most four-wheel-drive vehicles are very expensive. Thus, Subaru enjoys an effective monopoly in its product/market and garners almost one-half of its American sales from this niche strategy.

CONCLUSIONS

Over the last twelve years the American market for Japanese and

German automobiles has seen great extension in the product/market diversity of the Japanese and German automanufacturers. Application of Howard-Harris clustering to the data revealed that the firms have generally preferred to flood established product/market groups with models. As the established groups became flooded, the producers offering models appealing to customers on the edges of macrosegments further differentiated their products, repositioning them to develop new product/market groups.

Analysis of the individual firms' product/market strategies revealed large differences in their past competitive behavior. Volkswagen, Toyota, and Nissan refought the 1920's contest between Ford and General Motors. Volkswagen, like Ford, held to a narrow product/market scope focused on one highly successful product. Toyota and Nissan, like General Motors, built from a moderately wide product/market scope to a very extensive one. Toyo-Kogyo, a late entrant, attempted to emulate Toyota and Nissan's wide scope strategies by building its product line quickly while adding the additional dimension of technological innovation. When its rotary engine sales collapsed, Toyo-Kogyo still maintained a wide product/market scope by introducing additional piston engine models. Porsche-Audi followed a succession of product/market strategies during the period. First, the company maintained the extremely wide but also disconnected scope resulting from Porsche-Audi's origin in merger. This scope was then reduced to two well-defined but separate groups of product/markets: Porsche sportscars and Audi sedans. Most recently, Porsche-Audi has reversed its retrenchment strategy and embarked upon a strategy of wider participation in each group of product/markets. Mercedes consistently followed a strategy of high pricing and extensive product/market scope, generally dominating its product/markets. Additionally, the firm has come to rely heavily on its diesel engines to maintain its unique position in the market. Bayerische Motoren Werke, a late entrant in the American market, based its penetration effort on a narrow product/market scope of sporty sedans. Gradually BMW has expanded this scope to include a greater number of models, but the firm has consistently maintained its basic strategy of concentration on sporty sedans. An even narrower product/market scope was established by another late entrant, Honda. Over most of the period, Honda sold only one model. This has recently been expanded to three highly similar products. However, Honda remained essentially true to its very highly focused product/market strategy. Subaru, a later entrant, attempted to emulate Honda's narrow product/market strategy. This was quickly changed, however, to a wider scope including two market niches. Subaru introduced a line of automobiles which, while lightly powered, were also low in price and weight. Additionally, the company produced a four-wheel-drive station wagon, the only such vehicle available in the United States.

When changes in the firm's product/market scopes are viewed in their entirety, the two national groups of firms exhibit very different characteristics. The German firms have gradually adjusted their product/market scopes to include heavier, higher-priced products with more powerful engines while eliminating their smaller, less expensive products. The Japanese, however, have developed product/market scopes which consistently include lighter, lower priced products with smaller engines and generally exclude more expensive and more massive products. Moreover, this separation of the national groups has increased markedly in recent years. The German and Japanese importers have, consequently, evolved into two separate sets of competitors offering different forms of product competition to domestic producers.

Figure 3-1

Dimensions of the Strategic Posture, Changes and Evolution Vectors

Vectors	Strategic Posture Vectors	Strategic Changes Vectors	Strategic Evolution Vectors
Elements	one per firm per year	one per firm per year	one per firm
Models	$\# \text{models}_T$	$\dfrac{\# \text{models}_T - \# \text{models}_{T-1}}{\# \text{models}_{T-1}}$	Average growth in # models
Product/Market Groups	$\# \text{groups}_T$	$\dfrac{\# \text{groups}_T - \# \text{groups}_{T-1}}{\# \text{groups}_{T-1}}$	Average growth in # groups
Ads	$\$ \text{advertising}_T$	$\dfrac{\$\text{advertising}_T - \$\text{advertising}_{T-1}}{\$ \text{advertising}_{T-1}}$	Average growth in $ advertising
Dealers	$\# \text{dealers}_T$	$\dfrac{\# \text{dealers}_T - \# \text{dealers}_{T-1}}{\# \text{dealers}_{T-1}}$	Average growth in # dealers
Prices	Price of most popular model$_T$ $(PMPM_T)$	$\dfrac{PMPM_T - PMPM_{T-1}}{PMPM_{T-1}}$	Average growth in price of most popular model

Figure 3-2

Plot of Within Group Variance vs.
the Number of Clusters 1965-1976

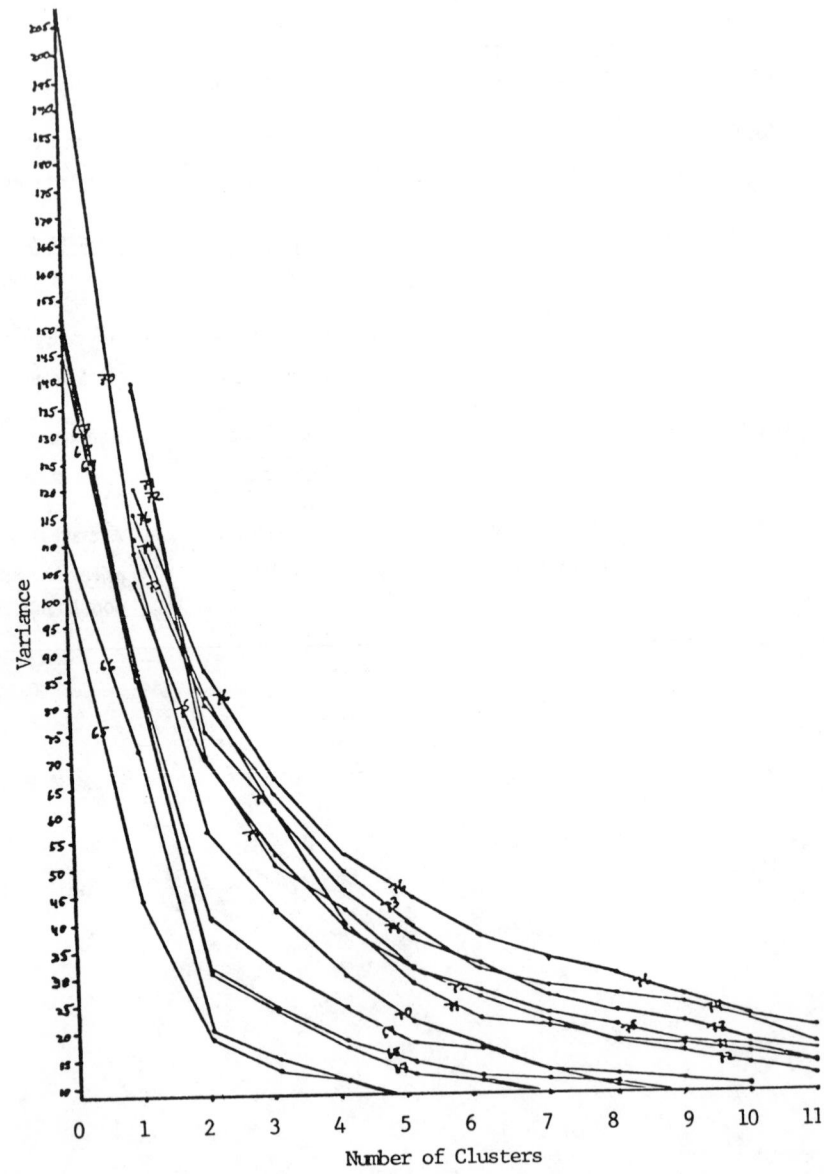

Figure 3-3

Biased F Values for Product/Market Clusters

Year No. Clusters	65	66	67	68	69	70	71	72	73	74	75	76
1												
2												
3	34.147	74.055	64.426	62.989	42.695							
4	12.122	9.807	9.860	11.491	11.038							
5	5.454	10.372	14.669	11.824	10.565		37.958					
6	11.688	9.227	15.438	11.067	13.982		26.899					
7	9.269	5.102	4.558	4.837	5.526	16.047	21.260	12.868				
8	3.402	6.572	9.897	4.376	7.776	16.103	6.904	14.399				
9			7.459	5.067	10.795	5.231	9.007	15.263				
10					5.566	8.754	5.178	8.414				
11					4.984	3.348	7.147	13.031				
12								13.906	15.299		11.627	8.774
13								5.637	8.158	10.146	6.760	10.146
14								6.827	7.430	10.662	7.861	9.502
15									8.237	4.176	6.905	5.406
16									13.291	9.104		5.399
17									8.700			

Figure 3-4

Total Number of Models,
Number of Product/Market Groups,
and Number of Firms vs. Time

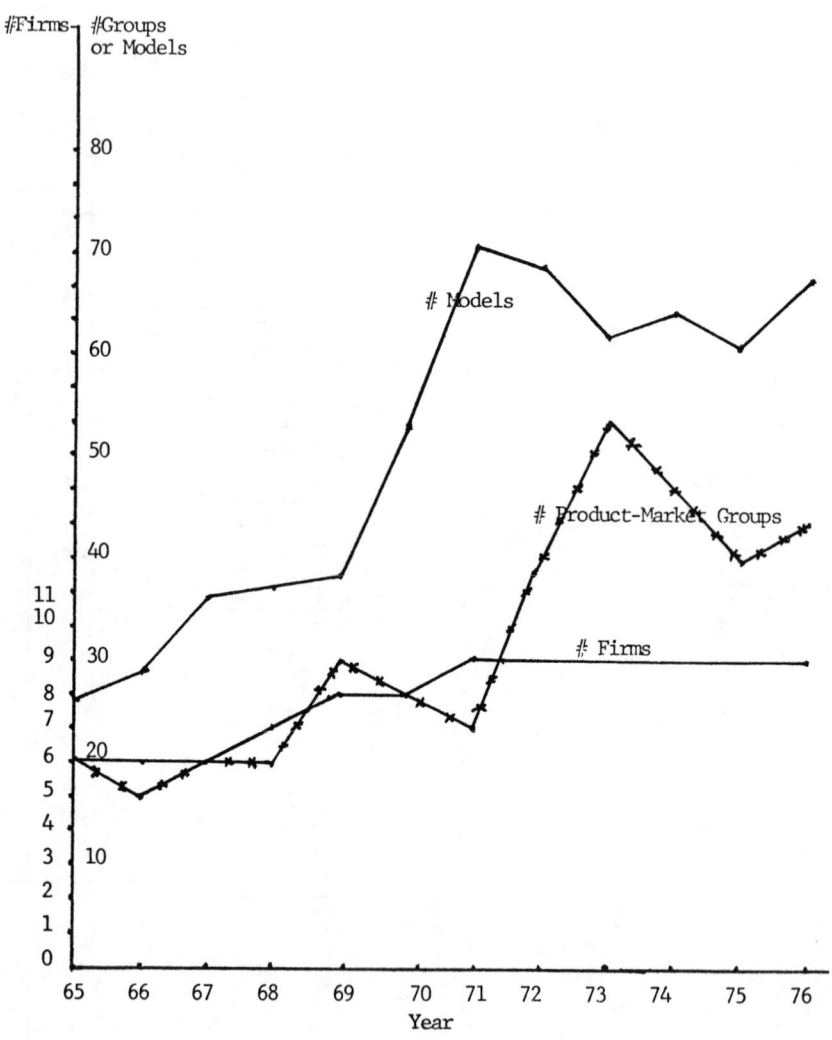

Figure 3-5

Number of Segments in Which Each
Company Competes — By Years

	65	66	67	68	69	70	71	72	73	74	75	76
VW	1	1	1	1	1	2	2	2	2	3	2	3
BMW	1	1	2	1	3	1	1	1	1	1	1	1
MB	4	3	4	4	5	5	4	5	4	4	4	4
PA	1	3	3	4	3	4	4	3	3	3	4	5
TY	3	3	3	4	4	3	3	2	4	3	3	5
TK	0	0	0	0	0	0	2	3	2	4	2	3
NI	3	2	2	2	1	2	3	3	4	3	4	4
HN	0	0	0	1	1	1	1	1	1	1	1	1
SU	0	0	0	0	1	2	1	1	1	1	1	1

Number of Models Offered by
Each Company — By Years

	65	66	67	68	69	70	71	72	73	74	75	76
VW	2	4	4	4	4	4	8	8	8	8	6	6
BMW	1	2	3	2	5	5	6	4	5	5	3	3
MB	8	7	10	9	10	11	11	11	8	8	10	10
PA	6	7	9	11	5	13	13	13	9	7	6	5
TY	4	4	4	6	7	10	14	9	12	13	12	12
TK	0	0	0	0	0	0	8	12	8	8	7	12
NI	5	4	6	4	5	6	7	6	7	10	10	10
HN	0	0	0	1	1	1	1	2	1	1	2	3
SU	0	0	0	0	1	3	3	3	4	4	5	6

Figure 3-6

Proportion of Years Each Pair of Firms Has Competed for One or More of the Same Segments

	VW	BMW	MB	PA	TY	TK	NI	HN	SU
VW		.417	.000	.750	.750	.667	.667	.111	.625
BMW	.417		.667	.583	.750	.833	.833	.000	.000
MB	.000	.667		.583	.583	.000	.417	.000	.000
PA	.750	.583	.583		.917	.833	.833	.222	.500
TY	.750	.750	.583	.917		1.00	1.00	.333	.375
TK	.667	.833	.000	.833	1.00		1.00	.500	.167
NI	.667	.833	.417	.833	1.00	1.00		.444	.125
HN	.111	.000	.000	.222	.333	.500	.444		.375
SU	.625	.000	.000	.500	.375	.167	.125	.375	

Figure 3-7

Average Number of Opposing Firms in Each Market Segment Addressed by Each Firm

	65	66	67	68	69	70	71	72	73	74	75	76	Aug.
VW	2.00	3.00	4.00	4.00	2.00	3.50	5.50	1.00	0.00	0.67	2.50	2.67	2.57
BMW	3.00	2.00	3.00	4.00	2.00	2.50	3.00	2.50	1.00	1.50	1.50	2.00	2.33
MB	1.00	1.67	1.25	1.50	0.80	1.00	0.75	0.40	0.00	0.00	0.00	0.25	0.72
PA	0.00	2.00	2.33	2.50	2.00	2.75	3.50	1.67	0.67	1.00	2.25	1.80	1.87
TY	2.33	2.67	3.00	2.50	1.75	3.00	4.33	3.00	2.67	2.67	2.67	1.80	2.70
TK	—	—	—	—	—	—	5.50	2.33	2.25	2.25	2.50	2.33	2.86
NI	2.33	3.00	3.50	3.50	3.00	3.00	4.00	2.00	1.50	2.00	1.50	2.25	2.63
HN	—	—	—	1.00	1.00	1.00	6.00	0.00	2.00	3.00	0.00	2.00	1.78
SU	—	—	—	—	1.00	2.00	6.00	1.00	0.00	0.00	2.00	3.00	1.88

Figure 3-8

Product/Market Scope of the German and Japanese Automanufacturers as Defined by
Four Major Product Attributes and the Level of Choices Offered Among the Attributes

	Frame based on size of wheelbase		Weight based on unladen weight		Power based on brake horsepower		Price based on base retail price in dollars
	size	choices	weight	choices	power	choice	
Mercedes-Benz	consistently large	consistently wide	moderate to heavy, trending toward heavy	consistently wide	high, trending toward low to high	consistently wide	moderate to high, trending toward high
BMW	consistently medium	narrow, trending toward moderate	light, changing to moderate to heavy	consistently narrow	moderate, trending toward moderate to high	consistently narrow	moderate, trending toward high

Figure 3-8 (Continued)

Product/Market Scope of the German and Japanese Automanufacturers as Defined by Four Major Product Attributes and the Level of Choices Offered Among the Attributes

	Frame based on size of wheelbase		Weight based on unladen weight		Power based on brake horsepower		Price based on base retail price in dollars
	size	choices	weight	choices	power	choice	
Porsche-Audi	small, trending toward small to medium	wide, trending toward moderate	very light, trending toward light to moderate	wide, trending toward moderate	low to moderate to very high	consistently wide	low to moderate, changing to moderate to high
Volkswagen	consistently small	narrow, trending toward moderate	light, trending toward light to moderate	narrow, trending toward moderate	low, trending toward low to moderate	narrow, trending toward moderate	low, trending toward moderate
Toyota	small, trending toward small to medium	moderate trending toward wide	moderate trending toward moderate to heavy	moderate trending toward very wide	consistently moderate	consistently moderate	low, trending toward moderate
Nissan	small, trending toward small to medium	moderate trending toward wide	consistently light to moderate	moderate trending toward wide	consistently moderate	consistently moderate	low, trending toward moderate to high

Figure 3-8 (Continued)

Product/Market Scope of the German and Japanese Automanufacturers as Defined by Four Major Product Attributes and the Level of Choices Offered Among the Attributes

	Frame based on size of wheelbase		Weight based on unladen weight		Power based on brake horsepower		Price based on base retail price in dollars
	size	choices	weight	choices	power	choice	
Toyo-Kogyo	consistently small	consistently narrow	consistently light to moderate	consistently very wide	consistently low to moderate	consistently moderate	consistently low to moderate
Honda	consistently very small	consistently narrow	consistently very light	consistently narrow	consistently low	consistently narrow	consistently low
Subaru	consistently small	consistently narrow	consistently light	consistently moderate	consistently low	consistently narrow	consistently low

IV

Strategies Employed to End Volkswagen's
Dominance of the U.S. Market
for Imported Automobiles

One of the most dramatic reversals of market dominance ever experienced in the automotive industry occurred in the market for imported automobiles in the United States in the middle 1970's with the abrupt collapse of Volkswagen's American sales. Why this collapse occurred, what strategies employed by Volkswagen's competitors helped to produce it, and why Volkswagen failed to foresee and prevent the collapse are all questions of prime importance in assessing recent corporate strategy in the U.S. market for imported automobiles.

In this chapter each of these questions is addressed. The chapter begins with an analysis of the strategic differences between Volkswagen and other German and Japanese automanufacturers. Volkswagen's strategic profile is compared with that of other firms as are changes in its strategy. The company's strategic profile and strategic changes are then examined in detail and compared with the corresponding strategic behavior of its two closest competitors, Toyota and Nissan.

METHOD OF ANALYSIS

The method of analysis employed here to compare and contrast the strategies of Volkswagen and its principal competitors is discriminant analysis. Many authors have discussed methods of evaluating the significance of a discriminant analysis, among them Green and Carroll,[1] Bolch and Huang,[2] Cooley and Lohnes,[3] Tatsuoka,[4,5] and Green and Tull.[6] These authors propose a number of evaluative statistics including: Bartlett's V, Mahalanobis' D^2, Hotelling's T^2, and Wilks Lambda. This study reports what appears to be the most popular of these interrelated measures, Wilk's Lambda. Significance of Wilks Lambda is determined by computation of Bartlett's V based on the value of Lambda. This V statistic distributes approximately as a chi-square distribution. Therefore, this study also reports the approximate chi-square value and its associated level of significance for each Wilks Lambda.

Additionally, two statistics are provided in an effort to remedy weaknesses in evaluating a discriminant analysis solely on the basis of its statistical significance. As Tatsuoka[7] states, "High statistical significance does not necessarily imply a large magnitude of difference (or association, as the case may be)." He continues, "Even if the statistic V . . . is highly significant, it does not automatically guarantee that the predictor battery exhibits a high degree of differentiation among the several groups." As a measure of total discriminatory power, Tatsuoka suggests a multivariate extension of Hays[8] omega-squared. In line with this recommendation, omega-squared is reported for each discriminant function as a measure of the proportion of variability in the discriminant space attributable to group differences. The second issue in the evaluation of a discriminant analysis is that of statistical significance versus classification performance. In the opinion of Green and Tull,[9] "statistical significance is no substitute for operational significance; one should be guided by the classification accuracy." Consequently, the classification (confusion) matrix and its associated chi-square and significance values are reported for each discriminant analysis performed.

APPLICATION TO VOLKSWAGEN AND ITS COMPETITORS

In using discriminant analysis to differentiate between the strategy of Volkswagen and those of its principal competitors, the first step is to develop strategic profile vectors for each company. Following this the strategic profile vectors were separated into two groups. The first group contained those of Volkswagen, and the second contained those of all other German and Japanese manufacturers. Discriminant analysis was then performed on the two groups using SPSS subprogram DISCRIMINANT.[10] This procedure generated one discriminant function with the following test statistics:

Wilks Lambda	=	.42535
Chi-Square	=	35.47574
Degrees of Freedom	=	5
Probability of no group difference due to chance	=	.000

The separation index, discriminant criterion value, or eigen value of this function is 1.35099. Thus, the discriminatory power of the battery of predictor variables, omega squared, is .599. This indicates that 55.9% of the variability of the discriminant function is attributable to differences between the two groups. Alternatively, 55.9% of the variability in the discriminant space is relevant to group differentiation.

The discriminant function coefficients for the two groups of strategic profile vectors are shown in Table 4-1. Volume of advertising showed by far the highest discriminant function coefficient with all other variables having approximately equivalent absolute magnitudes. Therefore, the statistically significant discriminating variables are advertising and number of dealers.

Discriminant analysis of the strategic changes vectors provided one discriminant function having the test statistics:

Wilks Lambda	=	.89521
Chi-Square	=	3.59749
Degrees of Freedom	=	5
Probability of no group difference due to chance	=	.609

The eigen value of this function is .11705. Thus, 7.65% of the variability in the discriminant space is relevant to group differentiation. Coefficients of the function are given in Table 4-2.

To verify the discriminatory power of the discriminant function, subprogram DISCRIMINANT performs a classification of the objects used in generating the function. Actual and predicted classifications are tabulated and percentage correct, Chi-Square, and significance values are computed. For the Volkswagen versus other firms dichotomy, prior classification probabilities were set at .1111 and .8888 respectively, reflecting the differing sizes of the two groups used in the analysis.

Prediction results of discriminant analyses performed for the Volkswagen versus other firms question are presented in Tables 4-3 and 4-4. The function derived from the strategic profiles vectors classified 100% of the vectors correctly for a Chi-Square of 45.00 and a probability of this level of accuracy occurring by chance of 0.00%. The function discriminating between the strategic changes vectors was able to correctly classify 88.9% of the vectors while achieving a Chi-Square of 21.778 reflecting a significance level of 0.00%.

ANALYSIS OF FINDINGS

Volkswagen's competitors consist of a highly varied set of companies. However, as Figures 4-1 and 4-2 show, it is possible to derive functions which differentiate Volkswagen's strategic profile and changes vectors from those of Volkswagen's competitors.

Comparison of Volkswagen's average position along each dimension of its strategic profile vectors with those of its competitors reveals that Volkswagen's position along the product dimension conforms almost perfectly to the average of its competitors. On the dimensions of distribution, price, and advertising, however, Volkswagen is vastly more competitive than the average. The data in Table 4-5 show that Volkswagen maintains over twice the average dealership network, prices its most popular model at one-half of the average price, and has advertised at four times the average of its competitors.

This stirring competitive effort on Volkswagen's part, therefore, begs the question of Volkswagen's drastic sales slide. Between 1970 and 1976 Volkswagen's American sales slid by 6.5% while total German and Japanese sales remained stable. This occurred while comparison with the overall averages showed Volkswagen to be a highly competitive company. The question remains, why? Two possibilities demand investigation. First, is Volkswagen's competitiveness truly as strong as it appears in comparison of its average position along each strategic dimension with the corresponding averages for the complete spectrum of German and Japanese automakers? Second, have there been changes in Volkswagen's competitive environment which have vitiated its efforts?

The statistics presented in Table 4-6 confirm the earlier judgment that Volkswagen is indistinguishable from the other firms in its number of models and number of product/market groups while holding a significant (.99 level) superiority in size of distribution network and in level of advertising. However, the difference in average prices is discovered to be statistically insignificant. The import of this is that no price advantage may be assumed for Volkswagen. Moreover, the large variance along the price dimension shown in Table 4-5, taken together with the importance of price in defining automotive product/markets, implies that Volkswagen's true competitors are not the whole set of German and Japanese companies, but rather a much more limited subset. Chapter IV reveals these to be primarily Toyota and Nissan.

Volkswagen's competitive environment changed in three significant ways during the period covered by this study. First, the overall competitive pace has quickened. More firms have entered the United States automarket (Honda in 1968, Subaru in 1969, Toyo-Kogyo in 1971) while the mean change along each dimension of the strategic changes vectors presented in Table 4-7 shows that competition along all strategic dimensions has become more vigorous. Tables 4-7 and 4-8 show that on the average Volkswagen's number of models, number of dealers, and level of advertising appear to be lower than the average of the other German and Japanese firms, while the average change in Volkswagen's price of its most popular model and number of product/market groups appears higher. Unfortunately, however, the variances along the dimensions of the changes vectors are so large that the only dimension displaying a statistically significant difference in its mean change is that of the number of dealers. On this dimension, Volkswagen has taken a clearly different path than the other firms, lowering its distribution slightly while the other firms were raising theirs.

Second, competition in Volkswagen's specific product/market groups has intensified drastically. In addition to the three new firms entering the market, all of whose offerings were, when introduced, aimed at Volkswagen's traditional low-price market, Volkswagen faced burgeoning competition from Toyota and Nissan. The new entrants have, of course, presumably drawn some sales from Volkswagen, but the major assault has been mounted by the major Japanese companies, Toyota and Nissan.

As the data presented in Table 4-9 show, Volkswagen's distribution network has shrunk in the face of its competitors' expansions. The price of its most popular model has risen far faster than those of its competitors, and the rise in its advertising volume has been far less than the rise in its competitors' volumes. In short, Volkswagen presents a picture of declining relative competitiveness.

Finally, the American public's long love affair with the Volkswagen Type 1 — the beetle, or the "bug" — ended. As Table 4-10 shows, the Type 1's sales, which were once the mainstay of Volkswagen's selling effort, have collapsed completely.

CONCLUSION

Having a model abruptly fall from favor is not unusual in the automotive industry. The important story is in Volkswagen's utter inability to generate an increase in sales of its other models. While the Type I's sales volume plunged 92% between 1971 and 1976, sales of Volkswagen's other models, which should have been increasing to replace the lost overall volume, were slipping 1%. Thus, Volkswagen lost its most popular model and was not capable of generating a new model or models at all able to quickly recoup the lost volume.

Volkswagen, a basically competitive company, has been beset by the triple pressures of overall increasing competitive effort on the part of all German and Japanese automakers, heavily enhanced competitive efforts from the major Japanese firms who compete directly in Volkswagen's product/market group and, finally, the utter collapse of the company's main product. These three interrelated occurrences combined to destroy Volkswagen's dominance of the market for German and Japanese automobiles and to reduce it to the status of one of a number of strong competitors.

Figure 4-1

Relative Location of Each Strategic Profile Vector and Group Centroid in the Discriminant Space Described by Discriminant Analysis of Volkswagen's Group of Strategic Profile Vectors and Those of the Other German and Japanese Automanufacturers

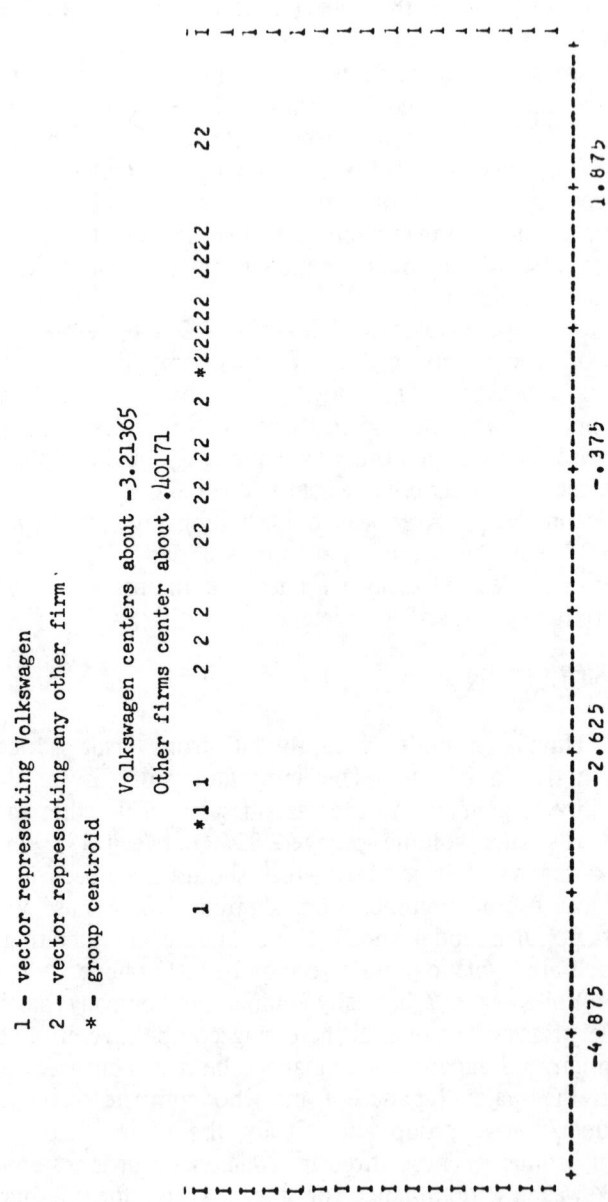

Figure 4-2

Relative Location of Each Strategic Changes Vector and Group Centroid in the Discriminant Space
Described by Discriminant Analysis of Volkswagen's Group of Strategic Changes Vectors and
Those of the Other German and Japanese Automanufacturers

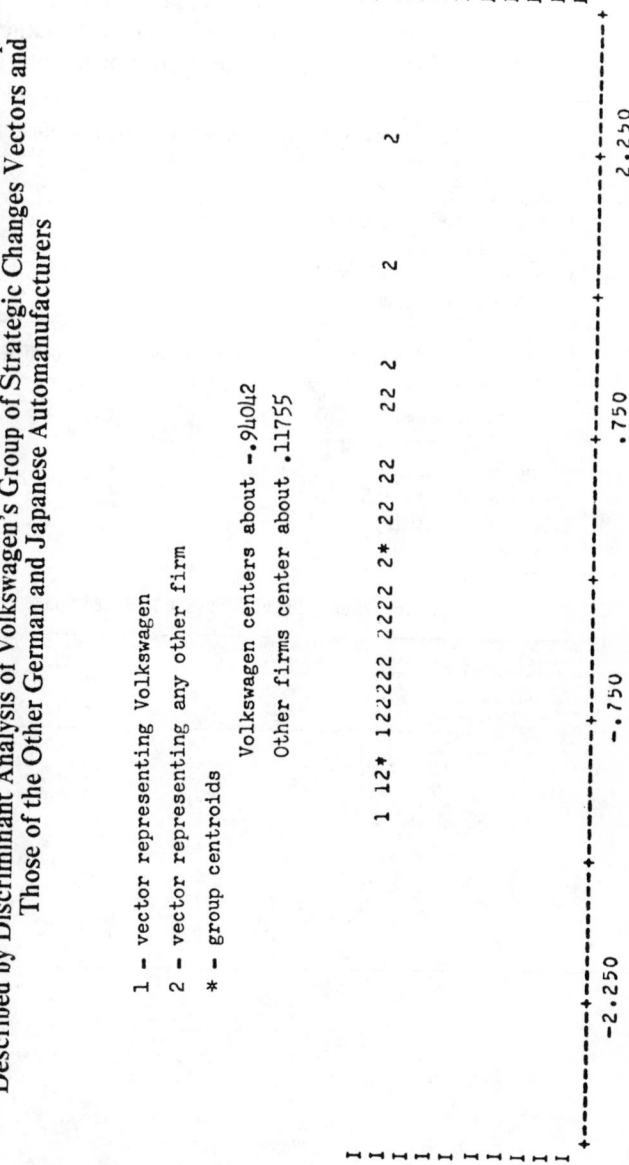

1 - vector representing Volkswagen

2 - vector representing any other firm

* - group centroids

Volkswagen centers about -.94042

Other firms center about .11755

Table 4-1

Results of a Discriminant Analysis Performed Between Volkswagen's Strategic Profile Vectors and Those of the Other German and Japanese Automanufacturers

Standardized Discriminant Function Coefficients	
Number of Models	.47955
Number of Product Groups	.53478
Number of Dealers	-.53513
Price of Most Popular Model	-.66664
Estimated Advertising	-1.44132

Unstandardized Discriminant Function Coefficients	
Number of Models	.141423
Number of Product Groups	.430175
Number of Dealers	-.161241E-02
Price of Most Popular Model	-.268322E-03
Estimated Advertising	-.171336E-03
Constant	1.52554

Centroids of Groups in Reduced Space	
Volkswagen	-3.21365
Others	.40171

Table 4-2

Results of a Discriminant Analysis Performed Between Volkswagen's Strategic Changes Vectors and Those of the Other German and Japanese Automanufacturers

Standardized Discriminant Function Coefficients	
Number of Models	.46227
Number of Product Groups	-.04815
Number of Dealers	.91408
Price of Most Popular Model	-.22660
Estimated Advertising	.07659

Unstandardized Discriminant Function Coefficients	
Number of Models	1.52437
Number of Product Groups	-.144662
Number of Dealers	4.89789
Price of Most Popular Model	-1.42386
Estimated Advertising	.100168
Constant	-.465053

Centroids of Groups in Reduced Space	
Volkswagen	-.94042
Others	.11755

Table 4-3

Classification Matrix Generated Using the Discriminant Function from the Discriminant Analysis Between Volkswagen's Strategic Profile Vectors and Those of the Other German and Japanese Automanufacturers to Predict Each Strategic Profile Vector's Group Membership

			Prediction Results	
Actual Group		Number of	Predicted Group Membership	
Name	Code	Cases	Volkswagen	Others
Volkswagen	1	5	5.0	0
			100.0%	0%
Others	2	40	0	40.0
			0%	100.0%

100.0 percent of known cases correctly classified
Chi-square = 45.000   Significance = .000

Table 4-4

Classification Matrix Generated Using the Discriminant Function from the Discriminant Analysis Between Volkswagen's Strategic Changes Vectors and Those of the Other German and Japanese Automanufacturers to Predict Each Strategic Changes Vector's Group Membership

Prediction Results

Actual Group Name	Code	Number of Cases	Predicted Group Membership Volkswagen	Others
Volkswagen	1	4	0 0%	4.0 100.0%
Others	2	32	0 0%	32.0 100.0%

88.9 percent of known cases correctly classified
Chi-square = 21.778   Significance = .000

Table 4-5

Means and Standard Deviations of the Dimensions for the Group of Strategic Profile Vectors for Volkswagen and for the Other German and Japanese Automanufacturers

Means

	Volkswagen	Others	Total
Number of Models	7.20000	7.15000	7.15556
Number of Product Groups	2.40000	2.70000	2,66667
Number of Dealers	1164.40000	531.92500	602.20000
Price of Most Popular Model	2664.20000	4234.10000	4059.66667
Estimated Advertising	24483.00000	7598.30000	9474.37778

Standard Deviations

	Volkswagen	Others	Total
Number of Models	1.09545	3.58451	3.39087
Number of Product Groups	.54772	1.30482	1.24316
Number of Dealers	63.81458	279.75332	331.88139
Price of Most Popular Model	606.09834	2577.88306	2484.48320
Estimated Advertising	3209.17941	6796.38785	8406.86999

Table 4-6

**Univariate Statistics Used in Comparing
Volkswagen's Strategic Profile Vectors to
Those of the Other German and
Japanese Automanufacturers Along
Each Strategic Dimension**

Wilks Lambda (U-Statistic) and Univariate F-ratio
with 1 and 3 Degrees of Freedom

Variable	Wilks Lambda	F
Number of Models	1.0000	.0009
Number of Product Groups	.9941	.2544
Number of Dealers	.6332	24.9141
Price of Most Popular Model	.9597	1.8071
Estimated Advertising	.5925	29.5687

Table 4-7

Means and Standard Deviations of the Dimensions of the Group
of Strategic Changes Vectors for Volkswagen and for the Other
German and Japanese Automanufacturers

Means

	Volkswagen	Others	Total
Number of Models	-.06250	.06132	.04756
Number of Product Groups	.16667	.09010	.09861
Number of Dealers	-.03033	.12983	.11204
Price of Most Popular Model	.15074	.11430	.11835
Estimated Advertising	.07221	.28969	.26552

Standard   Deviations

	Volkswagen	Others	Total
Number of Models	.12500	.31711	.30325
Number of Product Groups	.40825	.32905	.33284
Number of Dealers	.05071	.19009	.18663
Price of Most Popular Model	.03975	.16820	.15915
Estimated Advertising	.28196	.80433	.76461

Table 4-8

Univariate Statistics Used in Comparing Volkswagen's Strategic Changes Vectors to Those of the Other German and Japanese Automanufacturers Along Each Strategic Dimension

Wilks Lambda (U-Statistic) and Univariate F-ratio
with 1 and 34 Degrees of Freedom

Variable	Wilks Lambda	F
Number of Models	.9831	.5857
Number of Product Groups	.9946	.1837
Number of Dealers	.9252	2.7497
Price of Most Popular Model	.9947	.1821
Estimated Advertising	.9918	.2817

Table 4-9

1972 - 1976 Averages

Firm	Dealers	Price of Most Popular Model	Advertising
Volkswagen	1164	2664	24483
Toyota	952	2612	19956
Nissan	949	2763	17744

1972 - 1976 Total Percentage Growth (Diminution)

Firm	Dealers	Price of Most Popular Model	Advertising
Volkswagen	(12.0)	75.0	19.3
Toyota	14.2	50.8	40.3
Nissan	8.0	33.7	87.7

Table 4-10

Volkswagen Sales, 1971-1976

Year	Total Sales (1)	Type I Sales (2)	Other Sales (3)	(2) as % of (1)	(3) as % of (1)
1976	203234	27009	176225	13.3	86.7
1975	268751	92037	176714	34.3	65.7
1974	336257	243664	92593	72.5	27.5
1973	430602	372376	108226	77.5	22.5
1972	491742	360449	131293	73.3	26.7
1971	532904	354574	178330	66.5	33.5
Change					
1971-1976	-62%	-92%	-1%		

V

Similarities and Differences Among Strategies
Employed by German and Japanese Automakers

Volkswagen's dominance of the American market for imported automobiles was broken by the strategies of its competitors, German and Japanese, who competed directly and indirectly with it for sales in the import market segment. Of particular importance in Volkswagen's loss of dominance were the strong competitive efforts of the major Japanese firms who compete directly in Volkswagen's product/market group. This raises the second important research question: did Japanese and German firms, as groups, follow similar or different strategies in the U.S. market for imported automobiles?

This question is addressed in order to answer three more basic interrelated questions. First, are there national differences in international marketing strategy, specifically in the case of German and Japanese automakers? Second, in entering the American market, did the Japanese simply copy the strategies of the earlier German entrants, or did they follow other strategic approaches? Finally, are the strategies of the German and Japanese automakers tending toward similarity or toward dissimilarity?

RESULTS OF ANALYSES

Discriminant analysis of the strategic profile vectors generated one discriminant function with the statistics:

Wilks Lambda	=	.57958
Chi-Square	=	22.63612
Degrees of Freedom	=	5
Probability of no group difference due to chance = .000		

The function's eigen value of .72738 provides an omega squared indicating that 40.2% of the variability in the discriminant space is relevant to group differentiation.

Discriminant function coefficients for the two groups of strategic profile vectors are given in Table 5-1. These show price and advertising volume respectively to have the highest discriminatory power, followed by number of dealers and number of models. The most interesting result of the analysis, however, is that differences between the Japanese and Germans are so widespread. These two groups, which are almost always lumped together as "the import problem" or "the rising tide of automotive imports" are, in fact, vastly dissimilar in their competitive behavior. As the standardized coefficients of the discriminant function show, four variables representing all four basic dimensions of marketing strategy make substantial contributions to the discriminant function.

Discriminant analysis of the strategic changes vectors provides one discriminant function having the statistics:

Wilks Lambda	=	.77009
Chi-Square	=	8.49068
Degrees of Freedom	=	5

Probability of no group difference due to chance = 0.131

The function's eigen value of .29855 indicates that 20.3% of the variability in the discriminant space is relevant to group differentiation.

The discriminant function coefficients shown in Table 5-2 reveal that change in the number of models offered is the major difference between the two group's strategic changes vectors. In general, the German firms have significantly reduced their product lines while the Japanese have increased the number of their offerings.

Prediction results of discriminant analyses performed in addressing the Japanese firms versus German firms question are presented in Tables 5-3 and 5-4. The function derived from the strategic profiles vectors classified 77.8% of the vectors correctly for a Chi-Square of 13.889 and a probability of this level of classification accuracy occurring by chance of 0.00%. The function discriminating between the strategic changes vectors was able to correctly classify 75.0% of the vectors while achieving a Chi-Square of 9.000 and a probability of this performance occurring by chance of 0.03%.

ANALYSIS OF FINDINGS

The differing strategies employed by the group of German firms and the group of Japanese firms provide perhaps the most interesting question of the study as both groups have very successfully penetrated the American market. However, the foregoing analysis shows that the two groups have followed distinctly different strategies in penetrating the market.

Overall review of the presentations in Tables 5-1 through 5-8 and Figures 5-1 and 5-2 reveals the Japanese and German competitors to be remarkably alike in some respects, while remaining vastly divergent in others. The means and univariate F ratios presented in Tables 5-5 and 5-6 show that the means for the two groups differ significantly only on price (99% level) and number of product/market groups entered (90% level). Lack of homogeneity among the firms and among their chosen product/markets make it surprising that any significant univariate results were found. However, the two groups are distinctively different on the pricing dimension and are arguably different in the number of product/market groups in which they compete. Yet, as Figure 5-1 and Table 5-6 show, the strategic profiles of the German and Japanese firms differ sufficiently to allow ready separation into their actual groups. In fact, the centroids of the two groups in discriminant space are widely separated (Table 5-1). This results from the interaction of the dimensions in the formation of the discriminant function. While there are only two dimensions on which the two groups are different in a univariate sense, the German firms as a group and the Japanese firms as a group each exhibit a definite posture within the five dimensional strategic space. The discriminant function reflects all of the information contained in the data and is therefore capable of reflecting the joint effects of two or more variables in determining group membership.

When this was done, price and advertising were shown to be the most important predictors of group membership with number of models and number of dealers as secondary predictors (Table 5-1).

The data reveals each national group to be composed of two subgroups. The German firms behave as either specialty producers or as popular producers while the Japanese firms divide into established firms and recent entrants.

All of the German firms are consistent in pursuing higher priced markets than the Japanese. However, producers of the more luxurious or highly engineered automobiles such as the Mercedes, Porsche, Audi, or BMW display a strong tendency toward small distribution networks and limited advertising budgets. Volkswagen, in contrast, maintains the large distribution network and advertising budget of a producer of automobiles for a mass market. The German firms, as a group, are widely divergent in their product differentiation policies, ranging from the narrowly focused Bayerische Motoren Werke, which participates in few product/markets, to Daimler-Benz and Porsche-Audi, both of whom embrace a very wide variety of product/markets.

The Japanese firms are consistent in aiming their products at lower-priced markets than those addressed by the German firms. However, while all Japanese firms are comparatively lower in their prices, the rest of the firms' strategic postures appear to be determined by the time of their entry into the American market. Toyota and Nissan both exhibit the large dealership networks, high advertising expenditures, wide line of products and participation in a relatively large number of product/market groups characteristic of the established Japanese firms. Toyo-Kogyo, Honda, and Subaru, while also low in price, have moderate dealership networks and limited product offerings. Each of these firms occupies a very specific niche in the market. Honda produces and sells cars whose economy no other producer can equal. This is enhanced by Honda's development of the stratified charge engine used in its CVCC model. Subaru offers the American market its only four-wheel drive station wagon. Toyo-Kogyo, while listed as offering a fairly wide selection of models, is in reality a company offering a set of models with reciprocating piston engines and a set of models having rotary engines. The statistical procedures used in this study were not set to recognize the inherently similar factor differentiating rotary-powered Mazdas from other automobiles: the engine. Thus, Toyo-Kogyo's model selection is probably overestimated. Toyo-Kogyo appears to be a recent entrant which is trying to appear larger and more established than it really is. The size of Toyo-Kogyo's advertising expenditures reflects this view.

Review of the means of the dimensions of the strategic changes vectors presented in Table 5-7 reveals that the direction of movement in German and Japanese strategic behavior is very different. On the average, the Japanese firms have increased their number of models, number of product/markets entered and number of dealers far in excess of the corresponding German efforts along these dimensions. In pricing and advertising the status quo has been approximately maintained. As the low univariate F values in Table 5-8 show, however, concentration on the means is misleading. It was shown in chapter III and again, more definitively, here that most of the German and Japanese firms' competition comes from their own national groups and not from the other national group. Hence, the most interesting issue hinges on the performance of Volkswagen versus the Japanese firms. As the first research question demonstrated in detail, Volkswagen has not measured up to the aggressive efforts of its competition. When Volkswagen's rather poor showing is removed from the German group, the remaining German companies appear far more aggressive. However, close inspection of the Japanese firms' strategic changes vectors reveals the Japanese firms as far more aggressive in increasing their competitiveness than the German firms. Moreover, with the exception of Toyo-Kogyo, which has encountered financial difficulties, this increase in competitiveness extends to all of the Japanese firms. Figure 5-2 illustrates the large degree of dispersion among the firms' strategic changes vectors.

CONCLUSION

This section has shown the Japanese and German automanufacturers to be following very different strategies in penetrating the American market. The Japanese firms have been found to be aggressive competitors who are strengthening their position in the American market by attempting to utterly dominate the lower-priced mass merchandised product/markets. The German firms have also been shown to be aggressive competitors, but they have addressed other, higher-priced product/markets. Volkswagen, the German producer in closest direct competition with the Japanese firms, has been shown to be an anomaly among the German firms appealing, as it does, to a lower-priced mass market as opposed to the usual German products which are aimed at higher levels of the market. Close inspection of Volkswagen's recent behavior, however, reveals a pruning of its low priced lines, introduction of more advanced products, and a general upgrading of its technological image: in short, precisely the type of behavior which this study has found to characterize German firms. The new Japanese entrants to the market, in contrast, have entered with low-priced products, rapidly expanded their distribution and recently increased both their number of models and the number of product/markets in which they compete. In short, they are attempting to emulate the pattern which this study has found to be characteristic of the established Japanese firms.

Table 5-1

Results of a Discriminant Analysis Performed Between the German Firms' Strategic Profile Vectors and Those of the Japanese Firms

Standardized Discriminant Function Coefficients

Number of Models	.55331
Number of Product Groups	-.12922
Number of Dealers	.65045
Price of Most Popular Model	-1.27463
Estimated Advertising	-1.13263

Unstandardized Discriminant Function Coefficients

Number of Models	.163176
Number of Product Groups	-.103946
Number of Dealers	.195989E-02
Price of Most Popular Model	-.513035E-03
Estimated Advertising	-.134727E-03
Constant	1.28853

Centroids of Groups in Reduced Space

Japan	.74466
Germany	-.93082

Table 5-2

Results of a Discriminant Analysis Performed Between the German Firms' Strategic Changes Vectors and Those of the Japanese Firms

Standardized Discriminant Function Coefficients

Number of Models	-1.02461
Number of Product Groups	-.24184
Number of Dealers	-.59435
Price of Most Popular Model	-.36178
Estimated Advertising	.00469

Unstandardized Discriminant Function Coefficients

Number of Models	-3.37872
Number of Product Groups	-.726590
Number of Dealers	-3.18468
Price of Most Popular Model	-2.27324
Estimated Advertising	.613708E-02
Constant	.856537

Centroids of Groups in Reduced Space

Japan	-.47495
Germany	.59368

Table 5-3

Classification Matrix Generated Using the Discriminant Function from the Discriminant Analysis Between the German Firms' Strategic Profile Vectors and Those of the Japanese Firms to Predict Each Strategic Profile Vector's Group Membership

Prediction Results				
Actual Group		**Number of**	**Predicted Group Membership**	
Name	Code	Cases	Japan	Germany
Japan	1	25	22.0	3.0
			88.0%	12.0%
Germany	2	20	7.0	13.0
			35.0%	65.0%

77.8 percent of known cases correctly classified.

Chi-square = 13.889   Significance = .000

Table 5-4

Classification Matrix Generated Using the Discriminant Function from the Discriminant Analysis Between the German Firms' Strategic Changes Vectors and Those of the Japanese Firms to Predict Each Strategic Changes Vector's Group Membership

			Prediction Results	
Actual Group		Number of	Predicted Group Membership	
Name	Code	Cases	Japan	Germany
Japan	1	20	15.0	5.0
			75.0%	25.0%
Germany	2	16	4.0	12.0
			25.0%	75.0%

75.0 percent of known cases correctly classified.

Chi-square = 9.000   Significance = .003

Table 5-5

Means and Standard Deviations of the Dimensions of the Group of Strategic Profile Vectors for the German and for the Japanese Automanufacturers

Means

	Japan	Germany	Total
Number of Models	7.16000	7.15000	7.15556
Number of Product Groups	2.36000	3.05000	2.66667
Number of Dealers	665.12000	523.55000	602.20000
Price of Most Popular Model	2855.64000	5564.70000	4059.66667
Estimated Advertising	9689.40000	9205.60000	9474.37778

Standard Deviations

	Japan	Germany	Total
Number of Models	3.93362	2.66112	3.39087
Number of Product Groups	1.31909	1.05006	1.24316
Number of Dealers	273.77794	385.58206	331.88139
Price of Most Popular Model	661.37193	3074.12357	2484.48320
Estimated Advertising	7558.34829	9558.77272	8406.86999

Table 5-6

Univariate Statistics Used in Comparing the German Firms' Strategic Profile Vectors to Those of the Japanese Firms Along Each Strategic Dimension

Wilks Lambda (U-Statistics) and Univariate F-ratio with 1 and 43 Degrees of Freedom

Variable	Wilks Lambda	F
Number of Models	1.0000	.0001
Number of Product Groups	.9222	3.6273
Number of Dealers	.9541	2.0710
Price of Most Popular Model	.6998	18.4497
Estimated Advertising	.9992	.0360

Table 5-7

Means and Standard Deviations of the Dimensions of the Group of Strategic Changes Vectors for the German and for the Japanese Automanufacturers

Means

	Japan	Germany	Total
Number of Models	.14871	-.07889	.04756
Number of Product Groups	.12500	.06562	.09861
Number of Dealers	.14517	.07062	.11204
Price of Most Popular Model	.12200	.11378	.11835
Estimated Advertising	.23650	.30181	.26552

Standard Deviations

	Japan	Germany	Total
Number of Models	.34364	.18521	.30325
Number of Product Groups	.40329	.22447	.33284
Number of Dealers	.22403	.12002	.18663
Price of Most Popular Model	.16644	.15482	.15915
Estimated Advertising	.66449	.89572	.76461

Table 5-8

Univariate Statistics Used in Comparing the German
Firms' Strategic Changes Vectors to Those of the
Japanese Firms Along Each Strategic Dimension

Wilks Lambda (U-Statistics) and Univariate F-ratio with 1 and 34 Degrees of Freedom

Variable	Wilks Lambda	F
Number of Models	.8569	5.6759
Number of Product Groups	.9919	.2770
Number of Dealers	.9595	1.4358
Price of Most Popular Model	.9993	.0231
Estimated Advertising	.9981	.0631

Figure 5-1

Relative Location of Each Strategic Profile Vector and Group Centroid in the Discriminant Space Described by Discriminant Analysis of the German Firms' Group of Strategic Profile Vectors and Those of the Japanese Automanufacturers

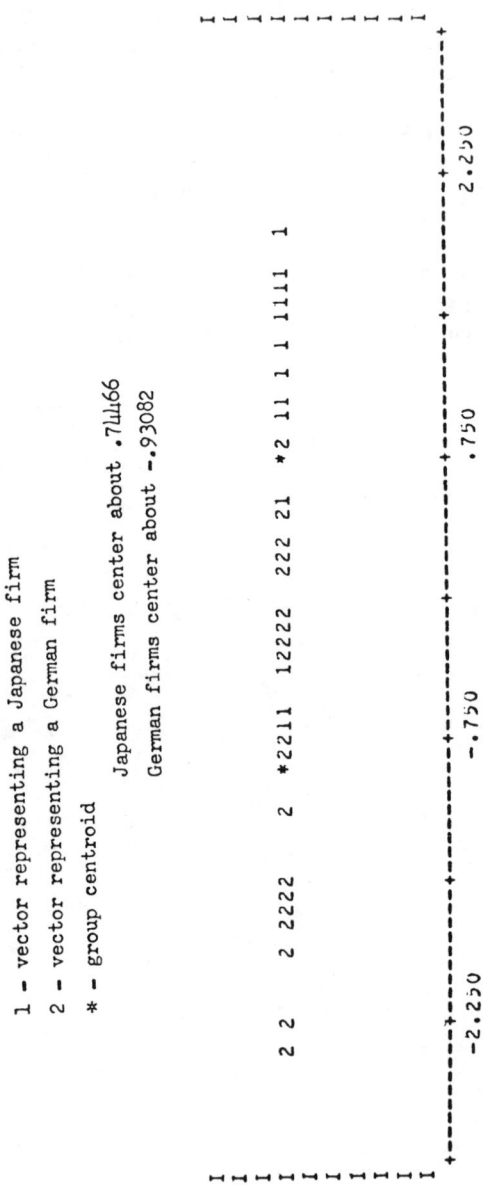

Figure 5-2

Relative Location of Each Strategic Changes Vector and Group Centroid in the Discriminant Space Described by Discriminant Analysis of the German Firms' Group of Strategic Changes Vectors and Those of the Japanese Automanufacturers

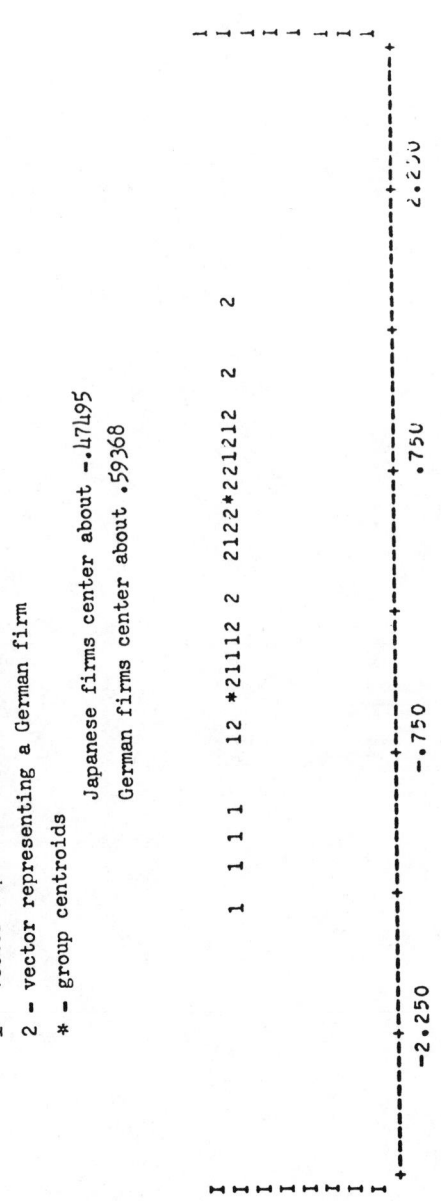

VI

Effects of Sales Volume on Corporate Strategy

A question of major interest in marketing strategy is the differences in strategies employed by high volume and low volume firms. In the U.S. market for imported automobiles there exists a marked difference in volume of sales between groups of German and Japanese firms. Volkswagen, Toyota, and Nissan have a high volume of sales in the United States; Bayerische Motoren Werke, Daimler-Benz, Porsche-Audi, Subaru, Toyo-Kogyo, and Honda all have a low volume of U.S. sales. Because each group is of mixed nationality, analysis of differences in strategies between the two groups is not concerned with national origin; rather, it seeks to identify patterns of strategic behavior common to higher or lower volume firms of both nations. Additionally, the analysis extends to examination of the changes in the strategies of higher and lower volume firms in an effort to discern whether the two groups are trending toward or away from one another in efforts to enhance their positions in the American market.

RESULTS OF ANALYSES

Discriminant analysis of the strategic profile vectors generated one discriminant function having the test statistics:

Wilks Lambda   = .10520
Chi-Square   = 93.45517
Degrees of Freedom   = 5
Probability of no group difference due to chance = .000

This function's eigen value is 8.50608, indicating that 89% of the variability in the group space is relevant to group differentiation.

The discriminant function coefficients for the two groups of strategic profile vectors are shown in Table 6-1. These reveal that number of dealers is by far the most important variable in differentiating between the two groups. Advertising volume, price level and number of product groups in which competition was offered were all of approximately equal importance and, surprisingly, were all of far lower weight in the function than was size of dealer network. A truly unanticipated result, however, was the low importance associated with the variable representing number of models. This was initially expected to be one of the distinguishing facets of a high volume producer. The analysis, however, shows that the two groups of producers are not distinguishable on that dimension.

Application of discriminant analysis of the strategic changes vectors of the two groups resulted in the generation of one discriminant function with the statistics:

Wilks Lambda	=	.81959
Chi-Square	=	6.46575
Degrees of Freedom	=	5
Probability of no group difference due to chance	=	.264

The eigen value of this function is .22012 indicating 15.3% of the variability in the discriminant space is relevant to group differentiation.

The standardized discriminant function coefficients shown in Table 6-2 reveal that the high volume producers are expanding their dealership networks at higher relative rates than are the low volume producers. On all other strategic dimensions, however, the two groups are essentially indistinguishable.

Prediction results of discriminant analyses performed for the high volume firms versus low volume firms question are presented in Tables 6-3 and 6-4. The function derived from the strategic profiles vectors classified 100% of the vectors correctly for a Chi-Square of 45.000 and a probability of this level of accuracy occurring by chance of 0.00%. The function discriminating between the strategic changes vectors was able to correctly classify 69.4% of the vectors while achieving a Chi-Square of 5.444 reflecting a probability of this performance occurring by chance of 2.0%.

ANALYSIS OF FINDINGS

When the materials in Tables 6-1 and 6-9 and Figures 6-1 and 6-2 are viewed in their entirety, an integrated picture of the strategic behavior of the high and low volume firms emerges. Some of this behavior is precisely as classical marketing theory would predict. Much, however, is unexpected, particularly in the evidence of short-term strategic maneuver reflected in the changes vectors.

The mean of each group's position along each dimension of its strategic profile vectors is given in Table 6-5. On the average, the high volume producers offer 50% more models than the low volume producers and do so in 29% more product groups. They maintain dealership networks two and one-half times the size of those of the low volume producers, advertise over four times as much, and price their most popular models at approximately one-half of the price of their lower volume competition. Generalizations based on averages are, however, dangerous. The univariate F ratios shown in Table 6-6 reveal that those relating to number of models and price of most popular model are particularly so. Close inspection of the data reveals that there is actually no generalizable picture of the model offering strategy of a low volume firm. Daimler-Benz (Mercedes) has consistently offered the widest selection of models among the German and Japanese firms. Toyo-Kogyo (Mazda), and Bayerische Motoren Werke (BMW) have persisted in offering a moderate level of selection relative to their competitors. Honda has rigorously restricted its product line while Subaru has extended its offerings from an original low level to its current moderate position. The picture of pricing strategies is equally blurred, however, for a different reason. In this case, the mean represents an average of two extremes. Daimler-Benz and Bayerische Motoren Werke represent prestigious cars and their products command commensurate prices. Honda, Subaru, and Toyo-Kogyo produce and sell low priced automobiles merchandised as basic transportation. An integrated strategic picture of the high and low volume firms is presented as Table 6-7.

There are no real surprises in the overall strategic picture of the high and low volume firms. However, analysis of the changes in the firms' strategic behavior does reveal a fascinating set of occurences. The data presented in Tables 6-8 and 6-9 reveal that each group has, on average, slowly increased the number of its models. However, the high volume firms have drastically increased the number of product/market groups in which they compete while the low volume firms have only slowly expanded into additonal product/market groups. This aggressive expansion on the part of the high volume firms results primarily from the efforts of Nissan and Toyota and is fully consistent with their behavior in their home market[1,2] and with the preemptive strategies employed by other large Japanese companies in the United States.[3,4] Relative to their initial positions, both sets of firms have implemented almost identical price increases, thus maintaining their relative positions along the pricing dimension of strategy. It is, rather, on the advertising and distribution dimensions that the low volume firms have attempted to increase their competitiveness. While the contributions of individual firms vary over the years, there has been an across-the-board jump in both measures in all of the low volume firms.

CONCLUSIONS

As is readily apparent in Figures 6-1 and 6-2, the strategic maneuvering has been both complex and confusing. This section has, however, developed an overall picture of the strategies employed by the high and low volume firms, and of the changes being effected in those strategies. High volume firms have been shown to be superior in their level of product/market group penetration, distribution, and advertising. While high volume firms offer large model selections, no overall picture of low volume firm performance on this dimension could be discerned. Pricing was shown to be a three-tier phenomenon with the high volume firms occupying the middle tier and low volume firms occupying both the higher and lower tiers. The high volume firms have been revealed as following strategies of product/market group expansion while the low volume firms have followed strategies of aggressive expansion of advertising and of distribution. Price and number of model offerings have proven to be dimensions along which the firms have selected to maintain a relative status quo.

Table 6-1

Results of a Discriminant Analysis Performed Between the Higher Volume Firms' Strategic Profile Vectors and Those of the Lower Volume Firms

Standardized Discriminant Function Coefficients

Number of Models	.05622
Number of Product Groups	.69210
Number of Dealers	2.08675
Price of Most Popular Model	-.48118
Estimated Advertising	.70690

Unstandardized Discriminant Function Coefficients

Number of Models	.165802E-01
Number of Product Groups	.556725
Number of Dealers	.628764/E-02
Price of Most Popular Model	-.193674E-03
Estimated Advertising	.840862E-04
Constant	-5.40007

Centroids of Groups in Reduced Space

Big	4.03188
Little	-2.01594

Table 6-2

Results of a Discriminant Analysis Performed Between the Higher Volume Firms' Strategic Changes Vectors and Those of the Lower Volume Firms

Standardized Discriminant Function Coefficients

Number of Models	.07879
Number of Product Groups	-.32599
Number of Dealers	.91089
Price of Most Popular Model	-.14205
Estimated Advertising	.11132

Unstandardized Discriminant Function Coefficients

Number of Models	.259813
Number of Product Groups	-.979417
Number of Dealers	4.88077
Price of Most Popular Model	-.892572
Estimated Advertising	.145591
Constant	-.395617

Centroids of Groups in Reduced Space

Big	-.64481
Little	.32240

Table 6-3

Classification Matrix Generated Using the Discriminant Function from the Discriminant Analysis Between the Higher Volume Firm's Strategic Profile Vectors and Those of the Lower Volume Firms to Predict Each Strategic Profile Vector's Group Membership

Actual Group		Number of	Predicted Group Membership	
Name	Code	Cases	Japan	Germany
Big	1	15	15.0	0
			100.0%	0%
Little	2	30	0	30.0
			0%	100.0%

Prediction Results

100.0 percent of known cases correctly classified

Chi-square = 45.000   Significance = .000

Table 6-4

Classification Matrix Generated Using the Discriminant Function
from the Discriminant Analysis Between the Higher Volume Firms'
Strategic Changes Vectors and Those of the Lower Volume Firms to Predict
Each Strategic Changes Vector's Group Membership

Prediction Results

| Actual Group | | Number of | Predicted Group Membership | |
Name	Code	Cases	Japan	Germany
Big	1	12	4.0	8.0
			33.3%	66.7%
Little	2	24	3.0	21.0
			12.5%	87.5%

69.4 percent of known cases correctly classified

Chi-square = 5.444   Significance = .020

Table 6-5

Means and Standard Deviations of the Dimensions of the Group of Strategic Profile Vectors for the Higher Volume and for the Lower Volume Automanufacturers

Means

	High	Low	Total
Number of Models	9.13333	6.16667	7.15556
Number of Product Groups	3.13333	2.43333	2.66667
Number of Dealers	1021.73333	392.43333	602.20000
Price of Most Popular Model	2679.60000	4749.70000	4059.66667
Estimated Advertising	19394.26667	4514.43333	9474.37778

Standard Deviations

	High	Low	Total
Number of Models	2.38647	3.41481	3.39087
Number of Product Groups	.91548	1.33089	1.24316
Number of Dealers	113.71359	155.93714	331.88139
Price of Most Popular Model	441.90607	2791.67373	2484.48320
Estimated Advertising	5534.54619	4012.00418	8406.86999

Table 6-6

Univariate Statistics Used in Comparing the Higher Volume Firms' Strategic Profile Vectors to Those of the Lower Volume Firms Along Each Strategic Dimension

Wilks Lambda (U-Statistics) and Univariate F-ratio with 1 and 43 Degrees of Freedom

Variable	Wilks Lambda	F
Number of Models	.8260	9.0559
Number of Product Groups	.9279	3.3391
Number of Dealers	.1829	192.1538
Price of Most Popular Model	.8422	8.0557
Estimated Advertising	.2880	106.3011

Table 6-7

Behavior of Each Firm Along Each Strategic Dimension

	No. of Models	No. of Product/Markets	No. of Dealers	Price of Most Popular Models	Advertising
Volkswagen	moderate	moderate	high	moderate	high
Daimler-Benz	high	high	low	high	low to moderate
Porsche-Audi	moderate	high	low	moderate to high	moderate
BMW	moderate	low	low	moderate to high	low
Toyota	high	high	high	low to moderate	high
Nissan	high	high	high	low to moderate	high
Toyo-Kogyo	moderate to high	moderate to high	moderate	low	moderate
Honda	low	low	grew from low to moderate	low	low to moderate
Subaru	moderate	low	moderate	low	low

Table 6-8

Means and Standard Deviations of the Dimensions of the Group of Strategic
Changes Vectors for the Higher Volume and for the Lower Volume
Automanufacturers

Means

	High	Low	Total
Number of Models	.05708	.04280	.04756
Number of Product Groups	.20833	.04375	.09861
Number of Dealers	.00771	.16420	.11204
Price of Most Popular Model	.11638	.11933	.11835
Estimated Advertising	.04317	.37670	.26552

Standard Deviations

	High	Low	Total
Number of Models	.18061	.35252	.30325
Number of Product Groups	.41363	.27810	.33284
Number of Dealers	.04113	.20898	.18663
Price of Most Popular Model	.11318	.18004	.15915
Estimated Advertising	.32245	.89512	.76461

Table 6-9

Univariate Statistics Used in Comparing the Higher Volume Firms' Strategic Changes Vectors to Those of the Lower Volume Firms Along Each Strategic Dimension

Wilks Lambda (U-Statistics) and Univariate F-ratio with 1 and 34 Degrees of Freedom

Variable	Wilks Lambda	F
Number of Models	.9995	.0173
Number of Product Groups	.9441	2.0127
Number of Dealers	.8393	6.5106
Price of Most Popular Model	.9999	.0027
Estimated Advertising	.9565	1.5459

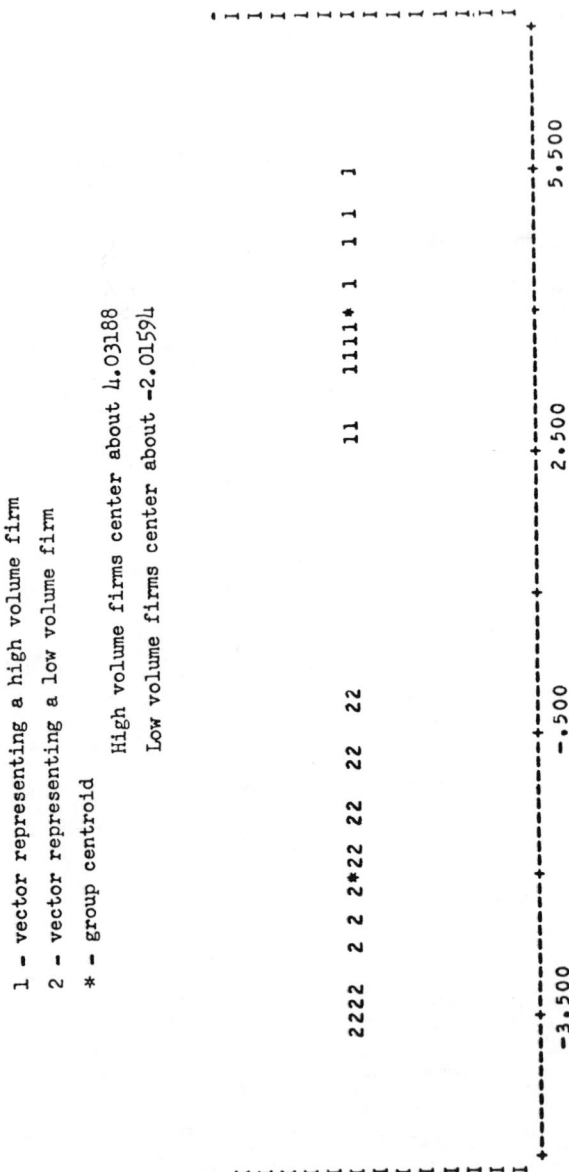

Figure 6-1

Relative Location of Each Strategic Profile Vector and Group Centroid in the Discriminant Space Described by Discriminant Analysis of the Higher Volume Firms' Group of Strategic Profile Vectors and Those of the Lower Volume Firms

1 - vector representing a high volume firm

2 - vector representing a low volume firm

* - group centroid

High volume firms center about 4.03188

Low volume firms center about -2.01594

Figure 6-2

Relative Location of Each Strategic Changes Vector and Group Centroid in the Discriminant Space Described by Discriminant Analysis of the Higher Volume Firms' Group of Strategic Changes Vectors and Those of the Lower Volume Firms

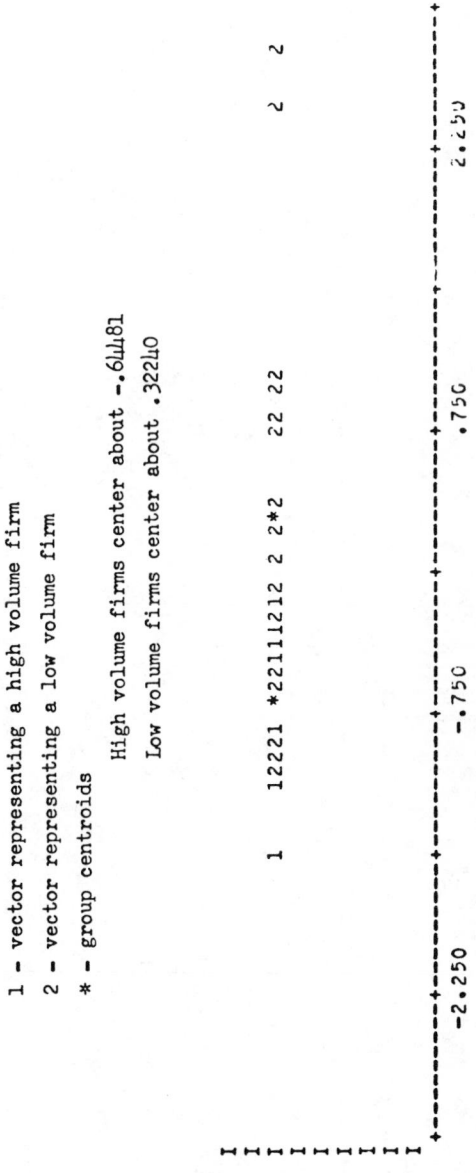

1 – vector representing a high volume firm

2 – vector representing a low volume firm

* – group centroids

High volume firms center about −.64481

Low volume firms center about .32240

VII

Strategy and the Marketing Mix

Differences in the marketing strategies employed by groups of Japanese and German firms were examined in Chapters IV, V, and VI. This chapter describes and contrasts relationships between strategic dimensions found in analysis of each group's marketing strategy.

INTERNAL CONSISTENCY IN CORPORATE STRATEGY

A basic tenet of corporate strategy is that to be successful, a firm's strategy must be internally consistent.[1,2,3,4] Competitive efforts made along one strategic dimension must be complemented by efforts along the others. Moreover, a change in position on any dimension may require corresponding changes in other dimensions in order to maintain the internal consistency of the firm's marketing strategy.[5] If a firm, or a group of firms, regards two strategic dimensions to be related in some competitive mix such that a certain position along one dimension will call for an additional complementary position along another strategic dimension, then the two dimensions will display a level of association reflecting the degree to which the firm, or the group of firms, links the two dimensions in the marketing strategy. Likewise, if two strategic dimensions are considered to be strongly linked, then a change in the firm's position along one dimension should be accompanied by a change in the firm's position along the other strategic dimension. Therefore, the changes in the firm's positions should be associated. One method of investigating association among variables is that of Pearson product-moment correlation. This procedure calculates the level of linear association between two variables, and is employed here to find such relationships between dimensions of the firms' strategies.

ANALYSIS OF FINDINGS

Three issues were addressed in Chapters IV, V, and VI: differences in strategic choice between Volkswagen and the other firms, between national groups, and between high volume and low volume firms.

Review of the within group correlation coefficients generated in this analysis and presented in Tables A-1, A-2, and A-3 reveals a pronounced similarity between the within groups correlation coefficients resulting from the comparison of Volkswagen's strategic profile vectors with those of the other firms and the comparison of the Japanese firms' strategic profile vectors with those of the German firms. However, the within groups correlation coefficients produced by these two groupings are vastly different from the within group correlation coefficients which were calculated from the comparison of the higher volume firms' strategic profile vectors with those of the lower volume firms.

While the close correspondence of the within groups correlation coefficients produced in the Volkswagen versus all other Japanese and German firms grouping and the Japanese versus German grouping can be readily explained by the fact that Volkswagen is a German firm and therefore its effect on the coefficients is subsumed within the group of German firms, this explanation will not explain the lack of similarity between the coefficients produced by comparison of Japanese firms' strategic profile vectors with those of German firms and comparison of higher volume firms' strategic profile vectors with those of lower volume firms. The group of Japanese firms contains both higher and lower volume companies as does the German group. Inversely, the group of higher volume firms contains both German and Japanese companies, as does the group of lower volume firms.

Linkage of Strategic Dimensions Among All Firms in the Study

Observation of the strong dissimilarity between the two different groupings of the same firms prompted calculation of the overall Pearson product-moment correlations shown in Table A-1. SPSS subprogram PEARSON CORR[6] was used in performing the analysis. This procedure computes the product-moment correlations for each variable and performs a test of statistical significance. These levels are reported in Table A-1.

The highest product-moment correlation given in Table A-1 is the value of .7841, produced by correlation of the strategic dimensions of advertising and number of dealers. This is followed by number of product/market groups with number of models at .6703, number of dealers with price of most popular model at -.4087, advertising with price of most popular model at -.3766, number of dealers with number of models at .2837, and number of product/market groups with advertising at .2469. While this plethora of significant correlation coefficients shows that the Japanese and German automakers evidently consider the dimensions of corporate marketing strategy to be substantially interrelated, the differences in the within group correlation matrices of Tables A-1, A-2, and A-3 were still unexplained. Therefore, four additional PEARSON CORR analyses were performed on the group of Japanese firms, the group of German firms, the group of higher volume firms and the group of lower volume firms. Results for the Japanese and German groups are given in Tables A-5 and A-6.

Linkage of Strategic Dimensions in the National Groups

The most highly correlated dimensions of the Japanese firms' strategic profiles are as follows:

number of product/market groups with number of models	.7995
advertising with number of models	.6748
advertising with number of product/market groups	.6569
advertising with number of dealers	.6081
number of product/market groups with number of dealers	.5366
number of models with number of dealers	.5064

The strongest correlations among the German firms' strategic dimensions were:

number of dealers with advertising	.9324
price with number of product/market groups	.6126
advertising with price	-.5965
number of models with number of product/market groups	.4681
price with number of dealers	-.4623

Comparison of the foregoing tables provides some intriguing insights into the differing German and Japanese perceptions of linkages between strategic dimensions. The Japanese firms link the two elements of product strategy, link level of advertising expenditures to the product and distribution dimensions, and associate level of product effort with level of distribution effort. The German firms, in contrast, display an incredibly high correspondence between their advertising and distribution efforts. Additionally, they strongly associate price with the number of product-market groups penetrated and, not surprisingly, display a moderately strong correlation, .4681, between the two elements of the product dimension. An interesting set of relationships, however, are those of price of most popular model with advertising and distribution. The German firms display a fairly strong pair of negative correlation coefficients, -.5965 and -.4623. The higher priced German firms tend strongly toward lower advertising levels and smaller dealer networks.

The Japanese display no such tendency. In contrast, the Japanese link advertising level to two of the three other strategic dimensions while the German firms link it positively to only one, but that very tightly. Both groups of companies associate number of product/market groups and number of models. This is, of course, not unexpected. However, the Japanese firms' correlation coefficient of .7995 is substantially larger than the German firms' coefficient of .6126.

Review of the Pearson product-moment correlation matrices for the strategic changes vectors of the Japanese and German automanufacturers given in Tables A-7 and A-8 reveals the greatest correlations among the Japanese firms' changes in their strategic dimensions to be:

advertising with number of dealers	.5405
price with number of models	-.5175
advertising with number of product/market groups	-.5054
number of dealers with number of product/market groups	-.3893
advertising with number of models	-.3409

The greatest correlations among the German firms' changes along their strategic dimensions were:

number of dealers with number of models	-.5728
advertising with number of models	-.3640
advertising with number of dealers	.3474

Inspection of the foregoing tables reveals that both groups of firms have been altering the direction of their strategies. The Japanese firms have maintained their moderately strong (.5405) correlation of advertising with the number of dealers, but have severely changed their linkage of a number of other dimensional pairs. Where advertising level was associated directly with both elements of the product dimension, number of models and number of product/market groups, their strategic changes have been a direct reversal of this, changing to -.3409 and -.5054 respectively. Likewise, they have reversed their stance on linking the number of dealers to the number of product/market groups, moving from a .5366 correlation among the strategic profile vector dimensions to a .3893 correlation among the corresponding dimensions of the strategic changes vectors. The German firms have also altered their strategies, albeit not as strongly as the Japanese companies. Their changes vectors reveal the German automakers to be continuing their direct association of advertising with number of dealers. However, the correlation of .3474 for the changes in the two dimensions is in no way as large as the .9324 shown in the profile vectors. Moreover, the German firms have maintained an inverse relationship between their changes in the number of models and both the number of dealers and the level of advertising. Interestingly, in the only two cases where the Japanese and German groups each show a positive correlation between two dimensions of their strategic changes vectors, the correlations are remarkably similar. The Japanese firms attained a correlation of .5404 between level of advertising and number of dealers compared to the Germans' .3474. Meanwhile, the German firms' correlation of -.3640 between advertising and the number of models was very close to the Japanese firms' correlation of -.3409.

Linkage of Strategic Dimensions in the Higher and Lower Volume Firms

While the differing propensities of the groups of Japanese and German firms to link their positions on strategic dimensions to their positions on other strategic dimensions has been explored, no consideration has yet been given to differences in the manner in which higher and lower volume firms associate their strategic dimensions. This is an important distinction because each volume group contains both Japanese and German firms yet, as the following analysis shows, their behavior in associating strategic dimensions is often dissimilar.

Four PEARSON CORR[7] analyses were performed to compute the Pearson product-moment correlations between dimensions of the strategic profile vectors and between dimensions of the strategic changes vectors of both the higher and lower volume groups. Results of this analysis are presented as Tables A-9, A-10, A-11, and A-12.

The strongest correlations between the dimensions of the higher volume firms' strategic profiles were:

advertising with number of product/market groups	-.5794
advertising with number of dealers	.5416
price with number of product/market groups	.5293
number of dealers with number of product/market groups	-.4614
number of product/market groups with number of models	.4490
number of dealers with number of models	-.3931

Corresponding correlations for the group of lower volume firms were:

number of product/market groups with number of models	.6816
price with number of product/market groups	.6767
price with number of models	.4065
advertising with number of models	.3737
number of dealers with number of product/market groups	-.3628
advertising with number of product/market groups	.3261

Comparison of these tables reveals that the higher and lower volume groups have largely associated position on the product/market groups element of product strategy with all four other dimensions. In most cases, the two groups have recognized similar associations. However, the lower volume firms show a markedly greater tendency to link the number of product/market groups to the number of models than do the higher volume firms .6816 to .4490. Moreover, while the higher and lower volume firms both connect advertising level and number of product/market groups, they reverse the connection. Higher volume firms recognized a strong negative correlation (-.5794) between the two dimensions while lower volume firms achieved a positive correlation of .3261. Additional higher volume firm associations were found betwen number of models and price of most popular model (.4065) and between number of models and level of advertising (.3737).

Correlation of the changes made by the higher volume firms along their strategic dimensions produced the following significant associations:

price with number of models	-.4608
advertising with number of product/market groups	-.4505

Changes along the strategic dimensions of the lower volume firms were found to have the following correlations:

advertising with number of dealers	.3901
advertising with number of models	-.3658
number of dealers with number of product/market groups	-.3458
price with number of models	-.3361
price with number of product/market groups	-.3058

The higher volume firms are moving to strengthen their inverse relationship between advertising level and number of product/market groups. Additionally, they are establishing an inverse connection between price of most popular model and number of models. Rather than ratifying their past courses of action, the lower volume firms have implemented extensive changes in associations between their strategic dimensions. Where the strategic profiles show a .6767 correlation between price of most popular model and number of product/market groups, the changes show a value of -.3058, a drastic reversal. The relationships between price and number of models and between advertising and number of models have been altered almost as abruptly, switching from .4065 and .3737 among the profiles to -.3361 and -.3658 among the changes respectively. Only in the case of the inverse relationship between number of dealers and number of product/market groups did the lower volume firms maintain their earlier level of association. In the sole case wherein both groups of firms exhibited a significant degree of correlation between two dimensions of strategic change, price and number of models, the lower volume firms altered their association of strategic dimensions to conform to the pattern of the higher volume firms.

CONCLUSIONS

The Japanese firms' marketing strategies contain a substantial relationship between the two elements of product/market scope, number of models and number of product/market groups, and level of advertising. A weaker relationship was found between advertising level and the number of dealerships. In developing their strategies, they have maintained the linkage between advertising and distribution dimensions while adjusting their prices and advertising inversely to changes in their product/market scopes.

The German firms, in contrast, have strongly associated the distribution and advertising dimensions while establishing an inverse relationship between advertising and price. They weakly link the two elements of product/market scope. In developing their strategies, they maintained their linkage of the advertising and distribution dimensions and varied both inversely with changes in their number of models.

Higher volume firms were found to have substantial relationships among the number of product/market groups and the strategic dimensions of advertising, price, and distribution. In developing their strategies, the higher volume firms continued their strong inverse relationship between advertising and the number of product/market groups while also linking price and number of models inversely.

Firms with lower sales volume displayed a very strong association between the two elements of product/market scope and price. A weaker relationship was found between level of advertising and number of models. Analysis of strategic development among the lower volume firms revealed substantial evidence of strategic change. Changes in the advertising and distribution dimensions displayed the strongest linkage while changes in advertising, distribution and price were all inversely related to changes in product/market scope.

VIII

Other Aspects of German and Japanese Strategic Behavior in the American Market

Groups of American firms following similar marketing strategies have been discovered by Hunt,[1] Newman,[2] and Porter.[3] The German and Japanese firms differ in nationality, sales volume, and product/market scope. However, a search for similarities among their strategies was conducted to identify common competitive behavior transcending these differences.

In this chapter the firms' strategic behavior is examined and four similar groups of firms are identified. Each group's common strategic behavior is then compared. The chapter concludes with a summary describing the three basic factors which allowed the German and Japanese automanufacturers to coalesce into four identifiable strategic groups.

METHOD OF ANALYSIS

Cluster analysis was performed on the strategic profile vectors and on the strategic changes vectors. Figure 8-1 illustrates the drop in unexplained deviation as the number of clusters was increased. As explained in Chapter III, if the clustering procedure were discovering valid relationships, the curves should be "L-shaped." It is readily apparent from the graphs that this is not the case. Application of Hartigan's[4] test for significance of clusters revealed that only four of the strategic profile clusters can be considered statistically valid. Unfortunately, no significant clusters could be generated from the strategic changes vectors. Analysis is therefore limited to consideration of the clusters of strategic profile vectors.

ANALYSIS OF FINDINGS

The four significant clusters generated from the strategic profile vectors are given in Table 8-1 with their standardized characteristics presented as Table 8-2. These reflect four basic modes of corporate competitive behavior: recent penetration with a limited product line, established penetration with a fairly wide product line and moderate prices, recovery from earlier competitive weakness with a wide product line, and established penetration with a highly priced very wide product line.

Recent Entrants

The first cluster contains all of the strategic profile vectors of Subaru, Bayerische Motoren Werke, and Honda, plus one early vector from Toyo-Kogyo. These firms followed strategies of low model selection within highly limited product/market scopes, moderate distribution, lower prices (with the exception of BMW) and low advertising expenditures. Only one vector from Toyo-Kogyo was included in the cluster, because 1973 was an unusual year for the company. In 1973, Toyo-Kogyo severely trimmed its product line. Thus, that particular profile was added to those of the narrow line companies.

One factor links the firms in this cluster: the short duration of their American penetration efforts. In each case, the firm entered the American market very recently or, as in the case of BMW, recently implemented a significant expansion of its penetration efforts. Therefore, the members of this cluster — Subaru, Honda and BMW — are styled the "recent entrants."

Established High Volume Firms

The second cluster contains the strategic profile vectors of Volkswagen, Nissan, and Toyota. These companies have fairly wide product lines focused on a moderate number of product/market groups occupying the lower to moderately priced part of the market for the German and Japanese automobiles. They have, by far, the largest dealership networks and are easily the highest volume advertisers. Each is a mass merchandiser of automobiles in its home country which has established a solid position in the higher volume sections of the American automarket.

Again, in this cluster, the firms are linked by a striking similarity in the duration of their American penetration efforts, all three firms having entered the American market prior to 1960. Additionally, all three firms' product/market scopes have been focused on lower to moderately priced high volume market segments. These firms are consequently styled the "established high volume firms."

Recovering Firms

The third cluster contains Porsche-Audi's strategic profile vectors, and also most of Toyo-Kogyo's.

Audi, division of Volkswagenwerk A.G., was formed by the merger of Auto-Union, NSU, and several small German ancillary companies. With the addition of a sales affiliation with Porsche, a joint sales arm, Porsche-Audi was born. Unfortunately, however, this company was charged with the responsibility of selling a disjointed line of automobiles running from the very spartan products of its NSU parent up to the luxurious and expensive Porsche Turbo Carrera. As Chapter III has already documented, Porsche-Audi has managed to come under competitive assault from every one of the other German and Japanese automakers. Porsche-Audi's response to this has been to drop out of the lower tiers of the marketplace, and to restructure its product line into what this study has found to be the stance of a typical German firm: heavier, larger, more quality-oriented products aimed at middle to upper socioeconomic groups.

Toyo-Kogyo is the other company contained in the third cluster. The last German or Japanese auto company to enter the United States, Toyo-Kogyo attempted to catch up through rapid expansion along all strategic dimensions and through reliance on its innovative rotary engine. (Interestingly, Porsche-Audi's precursor, NSU, built the first rotary-powered automobiles and still holds patents on the engine.) When the market for rotary-powered automobiles collapsed in the face of rising gasoline prices, only vigorous exertions on the part of the Japanese government and banking community prevented Toyo-Kogyo's financial collapse. Toyo-Kogyo has now resumed its penetration efforts, employing a product strategy of offering and advertising both its piston and rotary powered models. It has, however, confined its offerings to the lower to middle price ranges in what this study has found to be the characteristic posture of Japanese firms.

As a group, the firms in this cluster offer wide product lines in a relatively large number of product/market groups. In comparison with their competitors, their product's resale value is very low and their distribution networks are weak.

This cluster contains the troubled firms. In both cases, the companies encountered severe difficulty in penetrating the American market. Consequently, an underlying characteristic linking the two firms' strategies was their need to effect a competitive recovery. They are, therefore, styled the "recovering firms."

Market Dominants

The fourth cluster consists entirely of the strategic profile vectors of Daimler-Benz A.G., makers of the Mercedes. Mercedes represents a very special case among the German and Japanese automakers in that it seldom suffers very much direct competition from the others. In Chapter III it was shown that on the average Mercedes faces less than three-quarters of a competitor in each product/market group in which it competes. Most firms face an average of at least two. How does Mercedes manage this while offering the largest selection of models in an astounding number of product/markets through an extremely small distribution network at extremely high prices with minimal advertising? Close inspection of the data describing Mercedes' chosen product/markets provides the answer. The company is literally in a class by itself. It has selected to follow a strategy of utter dominance of a large set of small volume product/markets. In each product/market, Mercedes enjoys a relative monopoly, thus sustaining its profitability. However, the volume in each product/market is so low that were another competitor to consider penetrating it, he would face three dissuasive factors. First, the volume in each product/market is probably too small to support two profitable competitors. Therefore, the would-be aggressor would have to aim at domination of the product/market with the eventual aim of forcing Mercedes to withdraw from the product/market. Second, Mercedes now provides the established product in each of its product/markets. The marketing advantages of having an established product in a product/market are well documented and they would all accrue to Mercedes in any competitive duel. Finally, it has been demonstrated that costs go down as experience in a product/market rises. Mercedes has decades of experience in its product/markets and is presumably operating well down its cost curve, yet the annual sales volume in each product/market is so limited that any competitor attempting penetration would have to anticipate many years in which Mercedes would enjoy a substantial cost advantage. This would, moreover, allow Mercedes to lower its prices or to implement any other form of competitive retaliation which it felt would be effective.

Because of Mercedes' commanding position in its product markets, the cluster containing its strategic profile vectors is styled the group of "market dominants."

CONCLUSIONS

This chapter has described three additional relationships in the data which help to explain the competitive behavior of German and Japanese automanufacturers: date of market entry, need for competitive recovery, and product/market dominance. With these three factors, four strategic groups were identified. As Table 8-2 illustrates, the established firms,

Volkswagen, Toyota, and Nissan, followed common strategies emphasizing a moderate number of models and product/market groups, wide distribution, low prices, and high advertising. Bayerische Motoren Werke, Honda, and Subaru, the recent entrants, followed strategies of low model selection, moderately limited distribution, lower prices than their closest competitors, and low advertising. The recovering firms, Porsche-Audi and Toyo-Kogyo, offered wide product diversity through a limited distribution network at somewhat higher prices supported by moderate advertising expenditures. Mercedes-Benz, literally in a class by itself, implemented a strategy of market dominance by aiming a widely varied group of models at a highly defensible set of product/markets located socioeconomically above those of the other German and Japanese automanufacturers. This strategy featured highly restricted distribution of very high-priced products with minimal advertising effort.

The presence of both German and Japanese firms in each of the first three strategic groups shows that, despite the national differences in strategic behavior described in Chapter V, there are general strategic principals which transcend nationality. Firms occupying similar positions in the American market followed correspondingly similar strategies common to their strategic group.

Figure 8-1

Unexplained Sum of Squares Remaining at Each Level of Clustering of Strategic Changes Vectors, Strategic Profile Vectors

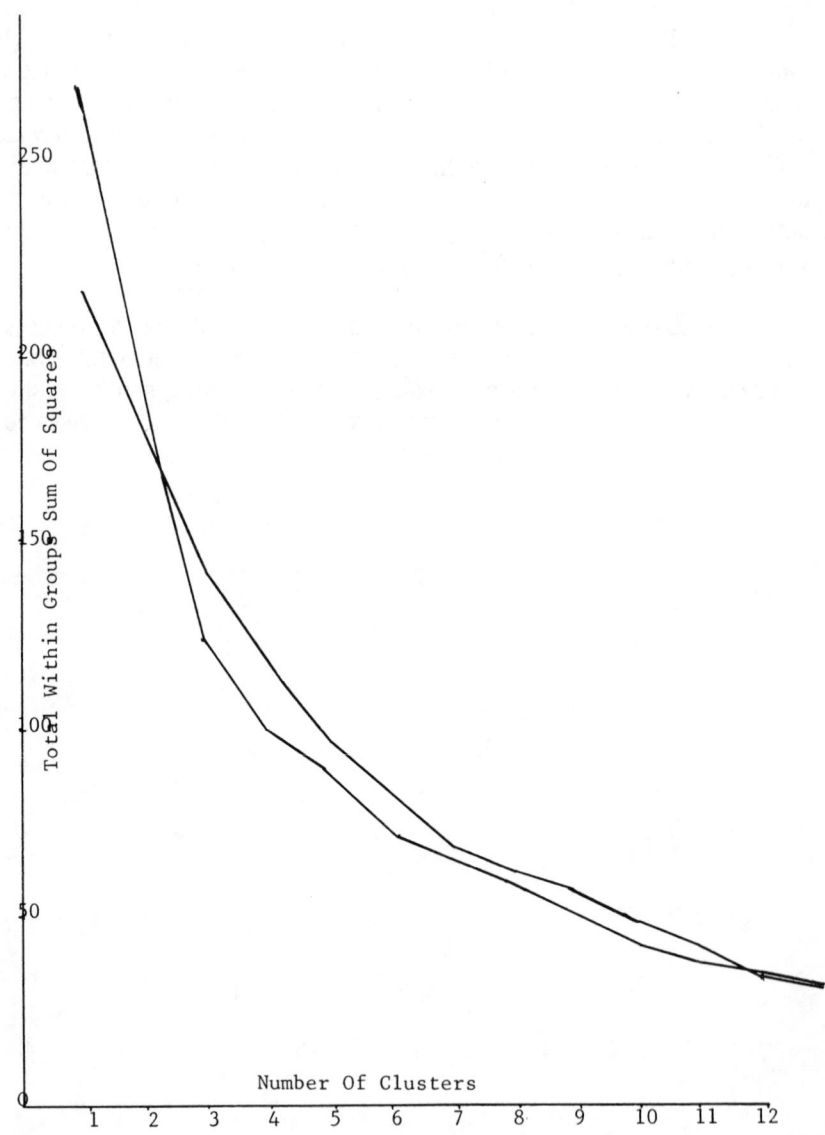

Table 8-1

Results of Clustering Strategic Profile Vectors Cluster Members

Cluster 1) recent entrants					
Subaru	1972,	1973,	1974,	1975,	1976
Toyo-Kogyo	1973				
BMW	1972,	1973,	1974,	1975,	1976
Honda	1972,	1973,	1974,	1975,	1976

Cluster 2) established firms					
Volkswagen	1972,	1973,	1974,	1975,	1976
Toyota	1972,	1973,	1974,	1975,	1976
Nissan	1972,	1973,	1974,	1975,	1976

Cluster 3) recovering firms					
Toyo-Kogyo	1972,	1974,	1975,	1976	
Porsche-Audi	1972,	1973,	1974,	1975,	1976

Cluster 4) Mercedes					
Daimler-Benz	1972,	1973,	1974,	1975,	1976

Table 8-2

Results of Clustering Profile Vectors
Standardized Cluster Characteristics

Cluster	No. of Models	No. of Product/Market Groups	No. of Dealers	Price of Most Popular Model	Advertising	Resale Price / List Price
1 Recent Entrants	-.364	-.370	-.189	-.081	-.288	.085
2 Established Firms	.129	.067	.311	-.141	.313	.046
3 Recovering Firms	.265	.316	-.279	.011	-.063	-.305
4 Mercedes	.669	1.247	-.678	2.476	-.765	.077

IX

Evaluation of Firm Strategies

Profitability is the ultimate measure of a firm's success in the marketplace. However, two factors prevent comparison of the profitability of Japanese and German penetration of the American automarket. First, unavailability of income statements reflecting the profitability of each firm's operations in the American market requires reliance on the firms' consolidated statements. However, the United States is only one of many markets penetrated by these firms and varies in its importance to each firm's global strategy. The differing American contribution to each firm's overall profitability, therefore, renders comparison of their consolidated statements useless in discovering the level of success of their American marketing strategies. Second, the accounting conventions applied to German and Japanese firms' public reports reflect the laws and business practices of their nations. Consequently, any comparison of reported profitability among the two national groups would be highly misleading in that it would involve comparison of figures of differing derivation.

Two measures of the success of a firm's strategy are available, however: effectiveness and efficiency. Effectiveness is measured in terms of the firm's number of unit sales per year, share of the total units sold by the Japanese and German automakers, and average annual rate of increase or decrease on each of these measures. Efficiency is gauged by analysis of the firm's average number of unit sales per dealer, average estimated number of dollars spent on advertising per unit sale, average number of sales per model, and the average annual rate of increase or decrease in each of these measures. This section evaluates each firm's ability to sell automobiles in the American market and the average level of marketing effort expended by each firm in achieving its sales. In the sections to follow, each automaker is evaluated as a member of one of the four strategic groups identified in Chapter VIII above.

ESTABLISHED HIGH-VOLUME FIRMS

Volkswagen, Toyota, and Nissan entered the American market in 1949, 1958, and 1959, respectively. Their strategies of moderately differentiated products with wide distribution, low prices, and high advertising have established them as volume leaders among the German and Japanese automanufacturers.

Effectiveness of the Established Firms

As a group, Volkswagen, Toyota, and Nissan have seen their collective share of market drop from 96% in 1965 to 74.4% in 1976. (Table 9-1) This collective lack of sales effectiveness is not, however, indicative of the overall performance of the established high-volume firms. Table 9-2 shows that during the decade Toyota raised its penetration from 1.55% to 31.07% while Nissan climbed from 4.35% to 27.44%. The overall average was depressed by the performance of Volkswagen, whose penetration collapsed from 90.1% of the Japanese and German penetration to only 15.91%.

Efficiency of the Established Firms

The sales success of Toyota and Nissan has been purchased at a stiff price. Tables 9-3, 9-4 and 9-5 show that the Japanese have consistently suffered fewer sales per model, fewer sales per dealer, and more advertising expenditure per sale than has Volkswagen. This reflects their aggressive strategy of rapid expansion of their model offerings, distribution, and advertising programs, as opposed to Volkswagen's relatively static strategy of relying on its older proven models sold through a static number of dealers with a high, but not an increasing, total level of advertising.

RECENT ENTRANTS

Subaru, Honda, and Bayerische Motoren Werke employed a varied set of strategies including moderate model selection, lower prices than their competitors, limited distribution, and low advertising. They differed, however, in the degree to which each firm emphasized each dimension in its overall marketing strategy. These differences are reflected in the firms' differing degrees of success in the American market.

Effectiveness of the Recent Entrants

As a group the recent entrants have been extremely effective in their penetration of the American market. Table 9-1 shows their share rising from 2.36% of the total Japanese and German penetration in 170 to 17.73% in 1976. The individual firms have all shared in this success, but to differing degrees. Honda, following a strategy of rapid expansion of its distribution network and advertising expenditures with the lowest prices among the Japanese and German producers and a very low degree of product differentiation, has surged from 0.37% of the total penetration in 1970 to 11.82% in 1976. Subaru, following a strategy of a static dealer network, low advertising expenditures and low to moderate prices with gradual expansion of the product line, achieved a fairly steady increase in its penetration, rising from 0.55% of the Japanese and German penetration to 3.83% in 1976. Tables 9-6 and 9-7 show a steady volume increase of approximately 57% per year with total sales rising from 5590 automobiles in 1970 to 48,928 in 1976. Bayerische Motoren Werke, in contrast to Subaru and Honda, has addressed a much higher socioeconomic stratum of the market. However, BMW has met with success in expanding its share of the American automarket, approximately doubling its U.S. sales between 1970 and 1976. The inherently low volume available from their product/markets has, however, restricted BMW's share of the German and Japanese total penetration to only 2%. The data in Table 9-6 reveal, moreover, that BMW's average yearly sales increase of 14% pales beside Subaru's 57% and Honda's 161%.

Efficiency of the Recent Entrants

The averages presented in Table 9-3 reveal that by implementing its strategy, Honda has achieved the highest level of sales per model of all the German and Japanese firms. This enviable position is the harvest from Honda's aggressive original investments in its market position. In the early 70's, Honda endured an unusually high level of advertising per sale and a very low level of sales per dealer. By 1976, however, Honda's advertising per sale was the lowest among the German and Japanese firms, while their average number of sales per dealer was the third highest. While the sales figures in Table 9-7 testify to some degree of effectiveness for their strategy, Subaru has not been able to spread its costs over the same volume as the more quickly growing Honda. Consequently, Subaru performs very poorly on the efficiency measures. Table 9-4 shows the firm's dealers enduring the lowest average level of sales per dealer among the German and Japanese firms. Moreover, the firm's average level of sales per model exceeds only those of troubled Toyo-Kogyo and the inherently low volume Mercedes and BMW: overall, a very weak performance.

While BMW's sales and strategic profiles are comparable to those of the other low volume competitors, BMW's performance on the efficiency measures is not directly comparable due to its different product/market orientation.   However, when compared to the other producers whose products appeal primarily to product/markets of limited demand (Mercedes and Porsche-Audi), Tables 9-3, 9-4, and 9-5 show Bayerische Motoren Werke having the lowest average sales per dealer, the second lowest (or second highest) advertising expenditure per sale, and the second highest average number of sales per model.   These figures reflect BMW's moderately aggressive approach to the American market and are reflected in its moderate sales growth rate.

DAIMLER-BENZ

As previously stated, Mercedes is, strategically, in a class by itself. The company has followed a strategy of targeting on the high quality, high price product/markets with moderate advertising expenditures, a restricted distribution network, and the highest prices of all German and Japanese producers.

Effectiveness of Daimler-Benz

This strategy has provided Mercedes with ten-fold growth in its unit sales during the decade 1965-1976. At its highest point, 1974, this sales volume reached 1562% of the 1965 level. Mercedes sales history, given in Table 9-7, follows an undulating pattern which now appears to have stabilized at approximately three and one half percent of the total German and Japanese penetration.

Efficiency of Daimler-Benz

Mercedes provides an excellent example of a firm whose strategy has shifted during the decade.   Mercedes has long provided a wide selction of high price, high quality automobiles. However, the company orignally sold its products through a very limited number of dealers and supported this effort with a minimal level of advertising. Mercedes sales increased at a declining rate throughout the late 60's with only gradual improvement in the company's average sales per dealer and average sales per model and with astonishingly low levels of advertising per sale. Beginning in 1970, however, the firm's advertising surged, distribution was broadened, and unit sales climbed.   By 1976 the company sold an average of 112 cars per dealer (compared with BMW's 90 and Porsche-Audi's 117), maintained an average level of advertising per sale, and had lifted the all-important average sales per model figure to three times its

1965 level. This last was a particularly signal accomplishment given the limited potential volume in Mercedes product/markets.

RECOVERING FIRMS

The recovering firms represent pathological cases among the Japanese and German automanufacturers. Porsche-Audi incorporates a participant of long standing in the American market, Porsche, and a relatively recent entrant, Audi. This combination originally encompassed a range of products extending from NSU super economy cars through Auto-Union sedans to sporty Porsches. This agglomeration was originally merchandised through a small number of dealers with a very limited level of advertising. In 1970, in the face of drastic contraction in their dealership network, Porsche-Audi reversed their strategy, increasing product offerings 260% and spending ten times as much on advertising as they had in 1969. Toyo-Kogyo presents the case of a recent entrant whose rise and fall were both meteoric. They approached the American market with the most aggressive strategy of all the German and Japanese firms. Exploiting the sales potential of its rotary engine, Toyo-Kogyo's strategy included rapidly expanding distribution, escalating advertising expenditures, increasing numbers of models and their degree of differentiation, and maintenance of prices in the popular moderate range. When sales of the firm's rotary-powered models collapsed in 1974, the company increased its advertising and distribution efforts while altering its product/market scope to include a wider variety of moderately priced piston-engined automobiles.

Effectiveness of the Recovering Firms

The recovering firms gradually increased their share of the Japanese and German penetration from a tiny 3% in 1965 to a respectable 11-13% in 1974-75. However, review of the sales data presented in Tables 9-1, 9-6, and 9-7 reveals that their progress has been both erratic and transient. In 1965, Porsche-Audi held 3% of the American market for Japanese and German automobiles.   By 1969, however, Porsche-Audi's sales had dropped to only 0.72% of the Japanese and German penetration. This precipitated their change to a considerably more aggressive strategy which resulted in five years of increasing sales. This recovery ended in 1975, however, with the company's sales plunging by one-third in 1976. Toyo-Kogyo's sales soared from 3098 in 1970 to 119,004 by 1973. Then disater struck; spurred by the Arab oil embargo, customer concern with fuel economy rose. Questions were raised regarding the economy of the rotary engine, and sales plummeted 37% in one year. By 1976, Toyo-Kogyo's share of Japanese and German market penetration had fallen to 3.22%; still respectable, but far from the 8.49% of 1973.

Efficiency of the Recovering Firms

In the late sixties, Porsche-Audi suffered the lowest number of sales per model of any German or Japanese firm in the American market: below even Mercedes, whose products compete in inherently low volume markets. Porsche-Audi's sales per dealer were easily the lowest among the German and Japanese importers, and its advertising per sale was approximately equal to Volkswagen's. The firm became more aggressive in 1970. However, the efficiency measures show that Porsche-Audi has been extremely erratic in implementing its newly aggressive strategy. The company accepted low levels of average sales per model and average sales per dealer with high advertising expenditures per sale in 1969-1970. However, as sales, sales per model, and sales per dealer rose, advertising per sale was reduced, and the flow of new models was first static and thence declined. In 1976, Porche-Audi again faced declining sales, resulting in its having the second highest per sale advertising among the German and Japanese firms, and maintaining an average number of sales per dealer less than one-half that of 1974.

Toyo-Kogyo entered the American market with a wide selection of models, but only average advertising effort per sale. Their small early distribution system achieved the second highest level of sales per dealer in their first year. The company then expanded rapidly, adding dealers and advertising to enhance its market share. This lowered the firm's efficiency slightly, but Toyo-Kogyo remained in the middle of the Japanese and German firms. In 1974, however, sales plunged, destroying the firm's product/market strategy and with it, the firm's marketing efficiency. By 1976, their large distribution system averaged only 79 sales per dealer, second worst of all the German and Japanese producers. Their wide line of products produced only 3432 sales per model, the worst Japanese or German performance, and their advertising level of $234 per sale dwarfed all but that of troubled Porsche-Audi, still a full $45 lower.

CONCLUSIONS

One common characteristic stood out when the firms' success in the American market was evaluated: aggressiveness. Consistently, firms following aggressive strategies were more effective, and eventually more efficient, than firms following less aggressive strategies. Among the established high volume firms, Volkswagen relied on its older products and static distribution network and was battered by the aggressive expansion of Toyota and Nissan. Honda, Subaru, and Bayerische Motoren Werke entered the market at approximately the same time, yet have not grown at the same rate. BMW, the least aggressive, has achieved the lowest rate of sales increase and generally the lowest efficiency. Honda, the most aggressive, had the highest effectiveness among the German and Japanese firms and has seen its costly early attempts to seize market share pay off in substantial recent gains in efficiency. Mercedes employed a steady progression of new products to dominate its product/markets, forestalling penetration by other competitors.

An aggressive strategy must, however, be consistently applied. Among the recovering firms, Porsche-Audi was ineffective until it adopted a more aggressive strategy.   When the firm faltered in implementing its new strategy, sales fell drastically.   Toyo-Kogyo aggressively penetrated the market and was phenomenally successful until consumer rejection of rotary engines crushed the firm's sales volume. Recent retrenchment of the firm's product, advertising, and distribution dimensions has been accompanied by a 41% sales drop (1975-1976) and a corresponding destruction of the firm's efficiency.

Table 9-1

Percentage of German and Japanese Penetration of the American Market Held by Each Class of Firm

	Established Firms	Recent Entrants	Recovering Firms	Mercedes
1976	74.42	17.73	6.96	3.48
1975	75.87	13.44	11.55	3.47
1974	79.89	7.46	13.79	3.65
1973	80.34	6.45	13.48	3.02
1972	84.88	5.20	8.91	3.33
1971	90.36	3.60	4.87	2.90
1970	93.21	2.36	2.35	2.88
1969	96.11	-	3.21	3.21
1968	95.65	-	3.31	3.31
1967	95.12	-	3.66	3.66
1966	95.55	-	3.29	3.29
1965	96.00	-	2.94	2.94

Table 9-2

Percentage of German and Japanese Penetration of the United States Market Held by Each Firm in Each Year

	Volkswagen	Porsche-Audi	Mercedes	Bayerische Motoren Werke	Toyota	Nissan	Toyo-Kogyo	Subaru	Honda
1976	15.91	3.74	3.48	2.08	31.07	27.44	3.22	3.83	11.82
1975	22.10	5.84	3.47	1.60	26.53	27.24	5.71	3.42	8.42
1974	31.57	6.74	3.65	1.38	25.29	23.03	7.05	2.16	3.92
1973	34.28	4.99	3.02	.97	23.31	22.75	8.49	2.70	2.78
1972	38.93	3.94	3.33	1.68	24.68	21.27	4.97	1.90	1.62
1971	44.01	3.18	2.90	1.64	25.55	20.80	1.69	1.17	0.79
1970	57.62	2.14	2.88	1.44	20.60	14.99	0.21	0.55	0.37
1969	69.49	0.72	3.21	—	15.96	10.66	—	—	0.00
1968	78.44	1.01	3.31	—	9.63	7.58	—	—	—
1967	80.35	1.18	3.66	—	6.73	8.04	—	—	—
1966	85.54	1.24	3.29	—	4.18	5.83	—	—	—
1965	90.10	1.12	2.94	—	1.55	4.35	—	—	—

Table 9-3

Average Number of Unit Sales Per Model

	Volkswagen	Porsche-Audi	Mercedes	Bayerische Motoren Werke	Toyota	Nissan	Toyo-Kogyo	Subaru	Honda
1976	33872	9558	4438	8836	33060	35040	3432	8155	50310
1975	44792	11827	4223	6473	26879	33120	9912	8318	51195
1974	42032	10262	4853	2939	20721	24527	9385	5745	41719
1973	60075	7767	5301	2726	27237	45572	14876	9448	38957
1972	61468	3826	3818	5309	34641	44778	5235	8019	10250
1971	66613	2960	3196	3304	22097	35989	2559	4705	9509
1970	145643	1662	2646	2917	20832	25252	–	1863	3772
1969	141589	1179	2619	–	18578	17377	–	–	65
1968	145502	678	2728	–	11911	14058	–	–	–
1967	113700	744	2069	–	9518	7582	–	–	–
1966	106924	885	2352	–	5227	7283	–	–	–
1965	185611	767	1515	–	1601	3585	–	–	–

Table 9-4

Average Sales Per Dealer for Each Firm in Each Year

	Volkswagen	Porsche-Audi	Mercedes	Bayerische Motoren Werke	Toyota	Nissan	Toyo-Kogyo	Subaru	Honda
1976	193	117	112	90	391	352	79	74	239
1975	229	230	105	65	331	349	131	56	184
1974	282	248	101	60	283	259	215	41	118
1973	399	267	114	61	351	342	379	62	139
1972	412	249	122	96	351	292	334	39	95
1971	459	279	115	90	356	280	—	34	—
1970	524	92	104	—	261	241	—	—	—
1969	532	25	97	—	182	143	—	—	—
1968	580	37	95	—	97	103	—	—	—
1967	480	—	81	—	65	84	—	—	—
1966	471	—	73	—	52	67	—	—	—
1965	439	—	36	—	19	—	—	—	—

Table 9-5

Estimated Advertising Expenditure Per Automobile Sold

	Volkswagen	Porsche-Audi	Mercedes	Bayerische Motoren Werke	Toyota	Nissan	Toyo-Kogyo	Honda
1976	140.34	188.82	75.42	96.68	70.44	68.99	234.05	52.78
1975	73.22	93.75	84.96	91.10	56.01	52.80	177.61	65.73
1974	76.36	139.88	87.16	27.22	72.69	82.32	111.82	88.69
1973	51.27	116.74	46.72	52.98	43.67	43.84	116.16	91.97
1972	48.60	124.70	77.96	27.36	63.87	47.94	104.33	49.95
1971	38.68	116.15	75.58	29.76	62.35	44.05	119.96	72.77
1970	31.88	152.83	112.48	30.31	66.42	46.49	42.90	129.90
1969	18.32	59.39	22.68	—	18.56	14.02	—	1215.38
1968	19.22	35.53	12.59	—	66.12	47.37	—	—
1967	22.50	16.72	10.00	—	56.65	4.46	—	—
1966	14.12	16.79	3.64	—	10.71	2.99	—	—
1965	18.53	19.13	34.17	—	12.18	2.73	—	—

Table 9-6

German and Japanese Unit Sales in the United States – Yearly Percentage Changes

	Volkswagen	Porsche-Audi	Mercedes	BMW	Toyota	Nissan	Toyo-Kogyo	Subaru	Honda
1976	-24	-33	5	37	23	6	-41	18	47
1975	-20	-1	9	32	20	35	-8	81	145
1974	-30	3	-8	8	-18	-23	-37	-39	7
1973	-2	41	1	-36	5	19	89	57	90
1972	-8	29	19	7	1	7	207	70	116
1971	-9	78	21	36	49	66	876	153	152
1970	3	267	11	*	60	74	*	*	570
1969	-3	-21	7	*	82	55	*	*	*
1968	28	11	19	*	88	24	*	*	*
1967	6	8	26	*	82	56	*	*	*
1966	15	35	36	*	226	63	*	*	*
1965	*	*	*	*	*	*	*	*	*
Average Annual Change (%)	-4	38	13	14	56	35	181	57	161

Table 9-7

German and Japanese Unit Sales in the United States

	Volkswagen	Porsche-Audi	Mercedes	BMW	Toyota	Nissan	Toyo-Kogyo	Subaru	Honda
1976	203234	47792	44376	26509	396723	350403	41179	48928	150929
1975	268751	70964	42232	19419	322553	331203	69384	41591	102389
1974	336257	71833	38826	14693	269376	245273	75079	22980	41719
1973	480602	69907	42405	13629	326844	319007	119004	37793	38957
1972	491742	49735	41998	21235	311770	268666	62818	24056	20500
1971	532904	38486	35156	19826	309363	251925	20474	14116	9509
1970	582573	21605	29108	14584	208315	151509	2098	5590	3772
1969	566356	5893	26193	*	130044	86883	*	*	65
1968	582009	7458	24553	*	71463	56233	*	*	*
1967	454801	6700	20691	*	38073	45491	*	*	*
1966	427694	6195	16465	*	20908	29131	*	*	*
1965	371222	4599	12117	*	6404	17923	*	*	*
Unit Sales Ratio									
$\frac{1976}{1965}$	0.55	10.39	3.66	---	61.95	19.55	---	---	---
$\frac{1976}{1970}$	0.35	2.21	1.52	1.82	1.90	2.31	19.63	8.75	40.01

X

Summary

This chapter summarizes the importance, purpose and scope of the study, the methodology applied in achieving the study's objectives, and the findings and conclusions which resulted. The chapter concludes with a discussion of the study's limits and directions for future research beyond these limits.

IMPORTANCE OF THE AUTOMOTIVE INDUSTRY
TO THE AMERICAN ECONOMY

The automotive industry is one of the largest and most important segments of the American economy. In 1975, the value of its production within the United States was over forty-five billion dollars, constituting three percent of the Gross National Product.[1] Over the past decade, direct production of automobiles has averaged approximately four percent of the GNP.[2] Mere production, however, considerably understates the impact on the American economy of its domstic automobile industry. In 1976, worldwide, the four major American automobile producers sold ninety-four billion dollars worth of products, earning a net income of 4.26 billion dollars and employing almost one and one-half million people,[3] of whom seven hundred and seventy-four thousand were employed in the U.S.[4] Further, these American jobs paid an average of one-third better than the average United States wage level.[5] Consequently, successful penetration of the domestic automobile market by Japanese and German automakers constitutes a direct threat to the well-being of the American economy and the American labor force.

PURPOSE OF THE STUDY

The purpose of this study was to describe, analyze, and evaluate the strategies employed by the Japanese and German automakers in penetrating the American market.

ES

dy addressed three specific research questions:

1. What strategies did the other German and Japanese automanufacturers, especially the Japanese, employ in ending Volkswagen's dominance of the U.S. market for imported automobiles?
2. Have Japanese firms and German firms, as groups, employed the same or different strategies in the U.S. auto market?
3. Have high volume firms employed a set of strategies that are significantly different from those of low volume firms?

Additionally, each firm's strategy was evaluated in terms of its success in the marketplace using both effectiveness and efficiency criteria. Finally, it is the nature of studies in corporate strategy to depart from basic hypotheses about corporate behavior in search of both the means of and reasons for that behavior. Consequently, this study was alert to the possible discovery of unanticipated behavior and results which were not incorporated in the initial research questions.

METHODOLOGY

Strategic theory defines the concepts of product/market scope, resource deployment, and specifications. Before analysis could proceed, however, it was necessary to define these underlying concepts in terms which are specifically relevant to the industry and firms to be analyzed: in this case, the Japanese and German companies who have attempted penetration of the American market for passenger automobiles. Moreover, it was necessary to specify the firms to be studied, the time period over which they were to be studied, and the dimensions upon which the firms' strategies were to be evaluated.

SELECTION OF FIRMS FOR STUDY

Studies in corporate strategy focus on the decisions made by firms' managements under certain environmental conditions. This study is an examination of the strategic decisions taken by top managers of German and Japanese auto manufacturers under conditions of increasing competition among themselves in penetrating the American market. Consequently, both the firms and the time period to be studied were selected to meet these requirements.

This study includes only those firms which are based and owned primarily in either Japan or West Germany and offer one or more passenger automobiles for sale within the boundaries of the United States. Further, the study extends solely to those market segments in which one or more Japanese or German automanufacturers offer a product. The firms meeting these criteria are:

1. Toyota
2. Nissan (Datsun)
3. Toyo-Kogyo (Mazda)
4. Honda
5. Subaru
6. Bayerische Motoren Werke (BMW)
7. Daimler-Benz (Mercedes)
8. Volkswagen (division of Volkswagenwerk)
9. Porsche-Audi (division of Volkswagenwerk)

Restriction of the study to these firms served three purposes:

1. The U.S. market for imported automobiles is essentially a Japanese and German one. Thus, the study included each firm's major imported competitors.
2. Restriction of the study to Japanese and German firms excluded fringe and transient competitors who were neither purposeful nor dedicated to penetration of the American market.
3. Since a basic purpose of the study was to analyze the competitive behavior of firms whose goals and strategies have been determined in foreign countries, the study excluded all foreign firms owned or substantially controlled by companies based in the United States on the ground that their goals and strategies are set for them by United States firms.

TIME PERIOD

The study examined the years 1966 to 1976 inclusive. This time period was chosen for two reasons:

1. During this period the Japanese manufacturers entered the U.S. market in strength and encountered an entrenched German presence. The differing initial market position of the two national groups, therefore, allowed comparison of their

subsequent strategic behavior resulting from their differing start-ing positions.

2. Extending the analysis backward beyond the mid 60's would have resulted in the inclusion of years in which there was either no direct competition or solely American competition with the German firms.   These relatively uncompetitive years would have conflicted with the overall purpose of the study which was to study foreign corporate behavior under conditions of foreign competition for a domestic market.

Two exceptions were made to this time specification.   First, if a given firm's competitive behavior appeared to reflect the influence of events which occurred prior to 1966, analysis of that firm's behavior was extended to include those earlier years necessary to understanding of the firm's later behavior.   Second, if a firm entered the American market after 1966, analysis of its competitive behavior commenced in the year of the firm's entry.

DIMENSIONS

Description of a firm's marketing strategy requires measurement of the firm's position along each of four dimensions: price, promotion, distribution, and product.   Measurement, in this study, was performed by a set of numeric control variables whose individual values described the firm's position along each dimension. Collectively, these control variables described the firm's strategic posture in each year.

The distribution dimension was measured by a variable representing the total number of U.S. dealers carrying the firm's products at year end.

The promotion dimension was measured by a variable representing the estimated yearly total number of dollars spent within the U.S. by a firm to advertise its products.   The value of this variable included spending on network and spot television, network and spot radio, bill-boards, and magazines.

Price was measured by two variables whose usage was determined by analytical purpose.   For purposes of product/market definition, price was measured by a set of variables whose values were the list prices of the firm's models at the yearly time of model introduction.   For purposes of strategic analysis, price was measured by a variable whose value was the price of the firm's most popular model in that year.   The firm's most popular model is that which achieved the highest number of unit sales in the year being described.

The product dimension was measured by a set of variables whose usage also was determined by analytical purpose. For purposes of product/market definition, products were described by a set of variables each representing a product attribute. Bulk was measured by the model's unladen weight in pounds. Physical size was measured by the model's wheelbase in inches. Power was measured by the maximum number of brake horsepower generated by the model's standard engine. For purposes of analysis of strategic evolution, the preceding product dimension variables for each year were replaced by two computed variables: the number of models produced in each year, and the number of market segments in which competition was offered.

DATA SOURCES

Values for each control variable for each firm in each year were drawn from the following data sources:

Values for the distribution dimension variable were calculated from yearly editions of *Ward's Automotive Yearbook.* Ward's compiles the number of retail outlets broken down by firm by state for each year. The value of the distribution variable for each year was computed by summing the values in that year for each firm.

Values for the promotion dimension variable were based on estimates of corporate advertising expenditures by Leading National Advertisers, Inc. These estimates have been compared with estimates provided by the Radio Advertising Bureau, Television Bureau of Advertising and the Outdoor Advertising Bureau and have proven consistent.

Values for the price dimension variables were taken from the introduction prices for each model from each firm as they appeared in the yearly issues of *The Automotive News Almanac.*

Values for the product attribute variables for each model from each firm were taken as they appeared in the "Product Specifications" section in yearly issues of *The Automotive News Almanac.*

DESCRIPTION OF STRATEGIES

As described in the strategic theory section (Chapter II), corporate strategies are multidimensional in scope. Consequently, in this study each firm's strategies were described by a set of vectors whose elements represented the firm's position or direction of movement along a strategic dimension.

The strategic posture vector is a five element vector describing a firm's position along each strategic dimension during one year. The five elements are:

1. The number of models offered for sale in the United States by the firm during the year
2. The number of product/market groups in which the firm's products competed during the year (Chapter III describes the computation of this variable)
3. The total number of dollars spent on advertising in the United States during the year
4. The number of dealers retailing the firm's products at the end of the year
5. The price of the firm's model achieving the highest level of sales in the United States during the year.

The strategic changes vector is based on the same five dimensions as the strategic posture vector. However, where the strategic posture vector represents a firm's absolute position on each strategic dimension during one year, the strategic changes vector represents the relative change in a firm's position along each strategic dimension betwen one year and the next. Thus, where the strategic posture vector reveals a firm's strategic position, the strategic changes vector reveals a firm's direction of strategic movement.

The final vector employed in describing each firm's strategy is the strategic evolution vector. This vector also consists of five elements representing the number of models, number of product/market groups, number of advertising dollars, number of dealers, and price of most popular model. However, rather than reflecting short-term position or direction, the elements of a firm's strategic evolution vector reflect the average annual change along each dimension during the period covered by the study. The evolution vector thus adds a long-term perspective to the information provided by the posture and changes vectors.

FINDINGS OF THE STUDY

Analysis of the strategies employed by the German and Japanese automanufacturers required investigation of five major areas: the degree to which firms compete with one another, the structure of their product/markets; differences in firms' strategic behavior, especially national differences, differences based on volume strategies, and differences between declining Volkswagen's strategies and those of its more successful rivals; strategic consistency, the degree to which firms recognized interrelationships among strategic dimensions; strategic groups, firms, following similar strategies; and evaluation of firm's strategies, the degree to which each firm effectively and efficiently penetrated the American market.

Product/Market Development Among the German and Japanese Automanufacturers

The data on number of models, number of product/market groups, and number of firms indicate that competition in the market has evolved in six distinct phases. The years 1965 to 1967 saw all six firms — Volkswagen, BMW, Mercedes-Benz, Porsche-Audi, Toyota, and Nissan — add models while essentially remaining in the same basic product markets. In the years 1967 to 1969, however, two new firms entered the market. Both Honda and Subaru followed a strategy of developing a new product/market group, that of the very small low-priced mini-cars. As Day and Shocker[6] would predict, this effort began with Honda's positioning of its first entry right on the edge of Porsche-Audi's weakest line, the NSU. By 1969, Honda and Subaru had each developed a separate product/market for their products. The years 1969 to 1971 were a period of heavy model proliferation without development of new product/market groups. Firms increased the number of models entered in their current groups and entered the groups which other competitors had already developed. While the number of models increased 87%, from 38 to 71, the number of product/market groups declined 23%, from 9 to 7. It was in the 1971 to 1973 period that development of new product/markets became fashionable in the industry. While each firm continued to compete in roughly the same number of product/market groups, and the total number of models offered actually declined, the market was shattered into over twice as many definable product/market groups, rising from 7 to 16. Where in 1971 it was not unusual for one group to contain half a dozen competitors, by 1973 no groups held more than three. 1973 to 1975 was another period of consolidation. The firms maintained their number of models. However, the models were repositioned to approach one fourth fewer product/market groups, dropping from 16 to 12. The data for 1975–1976 indicate that the firms resumed adding models. Moreover, Volkswagen, Porsche-Audi, Toyota and Toyo-Kogyo resumed adding product/market groups.

Within this product/market structure, individual firms were found to be following highly dissimilar product/market strategies in developing their product/market scopes. Volkswagen followed an extremely narrow strategy focused on exploitation of one highly successful product, the Beetle. Volkswagen revised its product/market scope only when sales of this product collapsed, and still competes in a very narrowly defined group of product/markets. Toyota and Nissan, in contrast, consistently maintained wide product/market scopes, each including several distinct product/markets. Toyo-Kogyo attempted penetration with a wide selection of products, many of them embodying a technological innovation, the rotary engine. When sales of these models collapsed, Toyo-Kogyo introduced additional piston-engined models to maintain its wide product/market scope. Porsche-Audi originally offered the widest selection of products among the German and Japanese automanufacturers. However, lack of a common approach to the market, a "common thread" linking their products, condemned Porsche-Audi to chronically low sales volume in most of its product/markets. The firm's strategy was then altered to conform to a much more restricted product/market scope focusing on moderately priced sedans and expensive sportscars. Mercedes-Benz consistently followed a strategy of wide model selection in a product/market scope focused on high quality and high prices. While still maintaining this basic strategy, the firm has gradually shifted its emphasis to include heavy reliance on a technological innovation, the diesel-powered sedan. Bayerische Motoren Werke, a far later market entrant than Mercedes, also followed a high quality, high price strategy. However, BMW always maintained a restricted product/market scope concentrating on more highly powered, sportier sedans. Honda, also a recent entrant, began its penetration with one model, the Civic. Gradually the firm has added models; however, its strategy of providing low-priced basic transportation has remained unchanged. The firm still adheres to the most narrowly restricted product/market scope among the German and Japanese importers. Subaru also entered the market with one model targeted at the basic transportation end of the market. Their product failed, however, resulting in a redefinition of the firm's product/market scope. Subaru introduced a line of products comparable in size to those of Toyota, Nissan, and Toyo-Kogyo but lighter, less powerful and at lower prices. The firm still follows this basic strategy of attempting to offer features beyond Honda's at prices below those of the other importers. Its most successful strategic effort, however, has been the firm's introduction of America's only low-priced four-wheel-drive station wagon. This niche strategy now provides one-half of Subaru's American sales.

Contrast Between Volkswagen's Strategies and Those of Its Competitors

Volkswagen was found to be a highly competitive firm with a wide distribution network, moderate prices, and an extremely high level of advertising effort. These competitive efforts were vitiated, however, by changes in Volkswagen's competitive environment and by the firm's inability to generate a popular new product to replace its declining older model, the "beetle".

Volkswagen's competitive environment changed in three significant ways. First, the overall competitive pace quickened. More firms entered the United States automarket (Honda in 1968, Subaru in 1969, Toyo-Kogyo in 1971). Moreover, analysis of changes in the firms' strategies revealed strong trends toward increasing competitiveness along all strategic dimensions.

Second, competition in Volkswagen's specific product/market groups has intensified drastically. In addition to the three new firms entering the market, all of whose offerings were, when introduced, aimed at Volkswagen's traditional low-price market, Volkswagen faced burgeoning competition from Toyota and Nissan. The new entrants have presumably drawn some sales from Volkswagen, but the major assault has been mounted by the major Japanese companies, Toyota and Nissan (see Table 4-9 and Table 4-10).

The tables illustrate that Volkswagen's distribution network has shrunk in the face of its competitor's expansions. The price of its most popular model has risen far faster than those of its competitors, and the rise in its advertising volume has been far less than the rise in its competitors' volumes. In short, Volkswagen presents a picture of declining relative competitiveness.

Finally, the American public's long love affair with the Volkswagen Type I — the beetle, or the "bug" — ended. As Table 4-10 shows, the Type I's sales, which were once the mainstay of Volkswagen's selling effort, have collapsed completely.

Having a model abruptly fall from favor is not unusual in the automotive industry. The important story is in Volkswagen's utter inability to generate an increase in sales of its other models. While the Type I's sales volume plunged 92% between 1971 and 1976, sales of Volkswagen's other models, which should have been increasing to replace the lost overall volume, were slipping 1%. Thus, Volkswagen lost its most popular model and was not capable of generating a new model at all able to recoup the lost volume quickly.

**Contrast Between the Japanese Firms' Strategies
and Those of the German Firms**

Both the Japanese and German firms have successfully penetrated the American market. However, they were found to have employed very dissimilar sets of strategies in achieving their penetration.

Each national group was found to be composed of two subgroups. The German firms behaved as either specialty producers or as popular producers while the Japanese firms divided into established firms and recent entrants.

All of the German firms were consistent in pursuing higher-priced product/markets than those of the Japanese. However, producers of the more luxurious or highly engineered automobiles such as the Mercedes, Porsche, Audi, or BMW displayed a strong tendency towards small distribution networks and limited advertising budgets. Volkswagen, in contrast, maintained the largest distribution network and advertising budget among the German and Japanese importers. The German firms, as a group, were found to be widely divergent in their product differentiation policies, ranging from the narrowly focused Bayerische Motoren Werke, which participates in few product/markets, to Daimler-Benz and Porsche-Audi, both of which embrace a very wide variety of product/markets.

The Japanese firms were consistent in aiming their products at lower-priced markets than those addressed by the German firms. However, while all Japanese firms were comparatively lower in their prices, the rest of the firms' strategic postures appeared to be determined by the time of their entry into the American market. Toyota and Nissan both exhibit the large dealership networks, high advertising expenditures, wide line of products and participation in a relatively large number of product/market groups characteristic of established Japanese firms. Toyo-Kogyo, Honda, and Subaru, while also low in price, have moderate dealership networks and limited product offerings. Each of these firms occupies a very specific niche in the market. Honda produces and sells cars whose economy no other producer can equal. This is enhanced by Honda's development of the stratified charge engine used in its CVCC model. Subaru offers the American market its only four-wheel drive station wagon. Toyo-Kogyo, while listed as offering a fairly wide selection of models, is in reality a company offering a set of models with reciprocating piston engines and a set of models having rotary engines. The statistical procedures used in this study wee not set to recognize the inherently similar factor differentiating rotary powered Mazdas from other automobiles – the engine. Thus, Toyo-Kogyo's model selection is probably overestimated. Toyo-Kogyo appears to be a recent entrant attempting to seem larger and more established than it really is. The size of their advertising expenditures reflects this view.

The strategies of the two national groups were also found to be evolving in different directions. On the average, the Japanese firms have increased their number of models, number of product/markets entered, and number of dealers far in excess of the corresponding German efforts along these dimensions, while maintaining the status quo in pricing and advertising. Concentration on the means, however, is misleading. Chapter III demonstrated that most of the German and Japanese firms' competition comes from members of their own national group and not from those of the other national group. Hence, the most interesting issue hinges on the performance of Volkswagen versus the Japanese firms. As the foregoing section demonstrated, Volkswagen has not measured up to the aggressive efforts of its competition. When Volkswagen's rather poor showing was removed from the German group, the strategies of the remaining German companies appeared far more aggressive. However, Japanese firms were still found to be substantially more aggressive in increasing their competitiveness than German firms. Moreover, with the exception of Toyo-Kogyo, which encountered financial difficulties, this increase in competitiveness was found to extend over all Japanese firms.

Comparison of the Lower Volume Firms' Strategies with Those of the Higher Volume Firms

Size of distribution network was found to be the strongest differentiating factor separating the higher and lower volume firms. Surprisingly, the data revealed that there is actually no generalizable picture of the model offering strategy of a lower volume firm. Daimler-Benz (Mercedes) consistently offered the widest selection of models among the German and Japanese firms. Toyo-Kogyo (Mazda), and Bayerische Motoren Werke (BMW) persisted in offering a moderate level of selection relative to their competitors. Honda rigorously restricted its product line while Subaru has extended its offerings from an original low level to its current moderate position. The picture of the lower volume firms' pricing strategies was equally blurred, but for a different reason. In this case, the mean represented an average of two extremes. Daimler-Benz and Bayerische Motoren Werke produce prestigious cars, and their products command commensurate prices. Honda, Subaru, and Toyo-Kogyo produce and sell low-priced automobiles merchandised as basic transportation.

In the development of their strategies, each group has, on average, slowly increased the number of its models. However, the high volume firms drastically increased the number of product/market groups in which they compete, while the low volume firms only slowly expanded into additional product/market groups. This aggressive expansion on the part of the high volume firms resulted primarily from the efforts of Nissan and Toyota and was fully consistent with their behavior in their home market[7,8] and with the preemptive strategies employed by other large Japanese companies in the United States.[9,10] Relative to their initial positions, both sets of firms implemented almost identical positions along the pricing dimension of strategy. It was, rather, on the advertising and distribution dimensions that the low volume firms attempted to increase their competitiveness. While the contributions of individual firms varied over the years, there was an across-the-board jump in both measures in all of the low-volume firms.

Strategy and the Automakers' Marketing Mixes

The Japanese firms' marketing strategies were found to contain a substantial relationship between the two elements of product/market scope – number of models and number of product/market groups – and level of advertising. A weaker relationship was found between advertising level and the number of dealerships. In developing their strategies, the Japanese maintained the linkage between the advertising and distribution dimensions while adjusting their prices and advertising inversely to changes in their product/market scopes.

The German firms, in contrast, were found to have strongly associated the distribution and advertising dimensions while establishing an inverse relationship between advertising and price. They weakly linked the two elements of product/market scope. In developing their strategies, the Germans maintained their linkage of the advertising and distribution dimensions and varied both inversely with changes in their number of models.

Higher volume firms were found to have substantial relationships among the number of product/market groups and the strategic dimensions of advertising, price, and distribution. In developing their strategies, the higher volume firms continued their strong inverse relationship between advertising and the number of product/market groups while also linking price and number of models inversely.

Firms with lower sales volume displayed a very strong association between the two elements of product/market scope and price. A weaker relationship was found between level of advertising and number of models. Analysis of strategic development among the lower volume firms revealed substantial evidence of strategic change. Changes in the advertising and distribution dimensions displayed the strongest linkage, while changes in advertising, distribution and price were all inversely related to changes in product/market scope.

Existence of Strategic Groups
Among the German and Japanese Automanufacturers

Three additional relationships in the data were found which helped to explain the competitive behavior of German and Japanese automanufacturers: date of market entry, need for competitive recovery, and product/market dominance. With these three factors, four strategic groups were identified. The established firms Volkswagen, Toyota, and Nissan, followed common strategies emphasizing a moderate number of models and product/market groups, wide distribution, low prices, and high advertising. Bayerische Motoren Werke, Honda, and Subaru, the recent entrants, were found to have followed strategies of low model selection, moderately limited distribution, lower prices than their closest competitors, and low advertising. The recovering firms, Porsche-Audi and Toyo-Kogyo, offered wide product diversity through a limited distribution network at somewhat higher prices supported by moderate advertising expenditures. Mercedes-Benz, literally in a class by itself, implemented a strategy of market dominance by aiming a widely varied group of models at a highly defensible set of product/markets located socioeconomically above those of the other German and Japanese automanufacturers. This strategy featured highly restricted distribution of very high priced products with minimal advertising effort.

The presence of both German and Japanese firms in each of the first three strategic groups showed that despite the national differences in strategic behavior described in Chapter V there are general strategic principles which transcend nationality. Firms occupying similar positions in the American market followed correspondingly similar strategies common to their strategic group.

Aggressive Strategies and Strategic Success

One common characteristic stood out when the firms' success in the American market was evaluated: aggressiveness. Consistently, firms following aggressive strategies were more effective, and eventually more efficient, than firms following less aggressive strategies. Among the established high volume firms, Volkswagen relied on its older products and static distribution network and was battered by the aggressive expansion of Toyota and Nissan. Honda, Subaru and Bayerische Motoren Werke entered the market at approximately the same time, yet have not grown at the same rate. BMW, the least aggressive, achieved the lowest rate of sales increase and generally the lowest efficiency. Honda, the most aggressive, had the highest effectiveness among the German and Japanse firms and has seen its costly early attempts to seize market share pay off in substantial recent gains in efficiency. Mercedes employed a steady progression of new products to dominate its product/markets, forestalling penetration by other competitors.

An aggressive strategy must, however, be consistently applied. Among the recovering firms, Porsche-Audi was ineffective until it adopted a more aggressive strategy. When the firm faltered in implementing its new strategy, sales fell drastically. Toyo-Kogyo aggressively penetrated the market and was phenomenally successful until consumer rejection of rotary engines crushed the firm's sales volume. Recent retrenchment of the firm's product, advertising, and distribution dimensions has been accompanied by a 41% sales drop (1975–1976) and a corresponding destruction of the firm's efficiency.

CONTRIBUTIONS TO STRATEGIC THEORY

The findings in this study contribute to a greater general understanding of three areas of corporate marketing strategy: nationality and strategic choice, strategic groups, and the role of aggressiveness in strategic success.

Nationality and Strategic Choice

Germany and Japan are two of the world's strongest industrial powers, each possessing a large, sophisticated domestic market and each highly successful in international markets. Both nations' automanufacturers successfully penetrated the American market, yet by different means. Japanese firms adopted product/market scopes encompassing high-volume markets. They followed low price strategies and expanded vigorously. The German firms, with the exception of Volkswagen, structured their product/market scopes around lower-volume markets. They followed higher pricing strategies and often attempted to dominate their product/markets. Volkswagen, the original exception to this pattern, has recently altered its strategy in the direction of the other German firms by introducing more highly styled, performance-oriented products at correspondingly higher price levels.

The definite pattern of similar competitive behavior found among each nation's firms and the strong dissimilarities between the competitive behavior of the two national groups revealed the strong effect of a firm's nationality on its international competitive behavior.

Strategic Groups

Groups of firms following similar strategies were found in the major appliance industry by Hunt,[11] in the chemical process industry by Newman,[12] and in retailing by Porter.[13] The strategic groups identified in this study extend the concept by illustrating that firms facing similar competitive conditions may adopt similar marketing strategies even though they compete in highly dissimilar product/markets and are of different nationalities.

Interaction of National and Strategic Groups

Each firm's strategic choices were made in response to two sets of environmental influences, those of the home country, and those of the American market. This resulted in each firm's strategy reflecting both the firm's national character and its position in the American market. Each set of influences is easily identifiable, yet the effects of each are tempered by the presence of the other.

Role of Aggressiveness in Strategic Success

Biggadike[14] found a strong relationship between the strength of a firm's competitive effort in penetrating a new market and the firm's resulting success or failure in the new market. A very strong relationship between the aggressiveness of firms' strategies for penetration of a new and foreign market (the United States) and their success in the market was found among the firms studied in this study. Universally, greater competitive efforts were associated with higher effectiveness in penetrating the market and with eventual higher efficiency. Reduction in competitive effort was associated with declining penetration and eventual lower efficiency. Therefore, Biggadike's linkage of competitive effort and success in penetration was found also to be true for foreign penetrators of the United States market, and Schwendiman's[15] recommendation of strong investment in market development was found to be not only good politics, but also good business.

DIRECTIONS FOR FUTURE RESEARCH

This study reports an investigation of the strategies employed by the Japanese and German automanufacturers in penetrating the American market. As such, it provides the basis for several additional investigations into the dynamics of corporate strategy. This is especially true in the areas of multinational marketing strategy, Japanese and German national industrial strategies, and strategic development in the automotive industry.

In the area of multinational marketing strategy, this study detailed the strategies by which Japanese and German automanufacturers penetrated the American market. The same firms constitute a large proportion of world competition in the automotive industry. Further research could readily extend the methodology of the study to analysis of the penetration strategies employed by all large automotive companies in penetrating the world's markets. This research would provide insight into the similarities and differences in penetration strategies employed by producers in entering differing national environments. Analysis of the effectiveness and efficiency of these strategies would add to understanding of the effects of national differences on strategic success and to their concomitant effect on strategic choice.

In its analysis of German and Japanese automotive firms' penetration of the American market, this study discovered a very distinct and different competitive style for each national group. This discovery, therefore, poses the question of whether there exist definite national differences in competitive behavior which transcend differences in industry. Again, the methodology of this study could readily be extended to analysis of the strategies employed by other Japanese and German firms in penetrating their sectors of the American market. Prime candidates for analysis among Japanese firms are provided by the electronics and photographic industries, while major German efforts have been evident in the drug and chemical industries. Research in this area would enhance understanding of long-term flows in world trade and might also help to explain the mechanism by which some countries are consistently strong competitors in world markets while others are generally weak.

This study has defined the basis for three further areas of research into the automotive industry: analysis of the American response to the German and Japanese challenge, and of the prospects for such response; analysis of automotive production strategies both within and without the United States; and, finally, analysis of the effects of American and world energy policies on the distribution of sales among the world's automobile producers.   Such research would be of particular value to American economic and energy planners as they attempt to formulate public policy in the areas of employment, energy use, and foreign trade.

Notes

CHAPTER 1

1. *Statistical Abstract of the United States 1976,* Bureau of the Census, United States Department of Commerce, Washington, D.C., table 989, p. 593.

2. Ibid.

3. "The Fortune Directory of the 500 Largest U.S. Industrial Corporations," *Fortune,* Vol. XCV, no. 5, May 1977, p. 366.

4. *Statistical Abstract of the United States 1976,* table 597, p. 378.

5. Ibid., table 605, p. 378.

6. "How the Japanese Blitzed the California Auto Market," *Forbes,* Sept. 15, 1971, pp. 28-29.

7. "New Car Sales Spurted by 12.5% in April from '76", *Wall Street Journal,* May 5, 1977, p. 7.

8. *Statistical Abstract of the United States, 1977,* table 1474, p. 867.

9. *Automotive Industries,* December 1, 1976, pp. 18, 24.

10. *Ward's Automotive Reports,* January 3, 1977, p. 4.

11. Leslie Darbyshire, *The Competitive Position of Imported Automobiles in the American Market,* DBA dissertation, Department of Finance, University of Washington, 1957.

12. Lawrence Jay White, *The American Automobile Industry in the Postwar Period,* Ph.D. dissertation, Department of Economics, Harvard University, 1969.

13. John R. Stuteville, "The Buyer as a Salesman," *Journal of Marketing,* Vol. 32, July 1968, pp. 214-18.

14. G.D. Bell, "Self-Confidence: Persuasion in Car Buying," *Journal of Marketing Research,* Vol. 4, February, 1967, pp. 46-52.

15. Edward L. Grubb, and Greg Hupp, "Perception of Self, Generalized Stereotypes, and Brand Selection," *Journal of Marketing Research*, Vol. 5, February, 1968, pp. 58-63.

16. F.C. Ahers, "Negro, White Autobuying Behavior: New Evidence," *Journal of Marketing Research*, Vol. 5, August, 1968, pp. 283-89.

17. Peter D. Bennett, and Robert M. Mandell, "Prepurchase Information Seeking Behavior of New Car Purchasers – The Learning Hypothesis," *Journal of Marketing Research*, Vol. VI, November, 1969, pp. 430-33.

18. Frederick Wiseman, "A Segmentation Analysis on Automobile Buyers During the New Model Year Transition Period," *Journal of Marketing*, Vol. 35, April, 1971, pp. 42-49.

19. F.K. Shuptrine, and G. Samuelson, "Dimensions of Marital Roles in Consumer Decision Making: Revisited," *Journal of Marketing Research*, Vol. XIII, Feb. 1976, pp. 87-91.

20. Gregory C. Chow, *Demand for Automobiles in the United States: A Study in Consumer Durables* (Amsterdam, The Netherlands: North Holland Publishing Company, 1957).

21. R.P. Smith, *Consumer Demand for Cars in the U.S.A.* (Cambridge, England; Cambridge University Press, 1975).

22. Frederic Stuart, ed., "Factors Affecting Determination of Market Shares in the American Automobile Industry," *Hofstra University Yearbook of Business*, Series 22, Vol. 3, October, 1965.

23. Frederick E. May, "Adaptive Behavior in Automobile Brand Choices," *Journal of Marketing Research*, Vol. 6, 1969, pp. 62-65.

24. "Japan: New Challenge to the U.S. in Autos," *U.S. News and World Report*, Vol. 65, August 5, 1968, pp. 63-64.

25. "Japan: Now Number 2 in Autos, Trucks and Going for Number 1," *U.S. News and World Report*, Vol. 68, June 1, 1970, pp. 42-43.

26. Ibid.

27. "Import U.S. Sales by Years," *Ward's Automotive Yearbook* 1974, p. 47.

28. Ibid.

29. *Statistical Abstract of the United States 1976*, table 19, p. 18.

30. "New Car Sales Spurted by 12.5% in April From '76," May 5, 1977, p. 7.

31. White, *The American Automobile Industry in The Postwar Period*, pp. 38-53.

32. "The Fortune Directory of the 500 Largest U.S. Industrial Corporations," p. 366.

CHAPTER 2

1. Alfred D. Chandler, Jr., *Strategy and Structure: Chapters In the History of American Industrial Enterprise* (Cambridge, Mass.: The MIT Press, 1962).

2. Russell L. Ackoff, "The Meaning of Strategic Planning," *McKinsey Quarterly*, Summer 1966, pp. 48-61.

3. Jack O. Vance, "The Anatomy of a Corporate Strategy," *California Management Review*, Fall 1970, pp. 5-12.

4. Alfred D. Chandler, Jr., *Strategy and Structure* (Cambridge, Massachusetts: The MIT Press, 1962).

5. Derek Channon, "The Strategy and Structure of British Enterprise," unpublished DBA thesis, Harvard Business School, 1971.

6. Gareth Dyas, "The Strategy and Structure of French Enterprise," unpublished DBA thesis, Harvard Business School, 1972.

7. Robert Pavan, "The Strategy and Structure of Italian Enterprise," unpublished DBA thesis, Harvard Business School, 1972.

8. Hernz Thanheiser, "Strategy and Structure of German Enterprise," unpublished DBA thesis, Harvard Business School, 1972.

9. Alfred D. Chandler, Jr., and Stephen Salsbury, *Pierre S. DuPont and the Making of the Modern Corporation* (New York, New York: Harper and Row Inc., 1971).

10. William Newman, "Strategy and Management Structure," *Proceedings, Academy of Management*, 1971.

11. Richard Rumelt, *Strategy, Structure, and Economic Performance*, (Cambridge, Mass: Harvard University Press, 1974).

12. Charles W. Hofer, "Some Preliminary Research on Patterns of Strategic Behavior," *Proceedings, Academy of Management*, 1973, pp. 46-54.

13. Schoeffler, R.D. Buzzell, and D.F. Heany, "Impact of Strategic Planning on Profit Performance," *Harvard Business Review*, March-April, 1974, pp. 137-45.

14. D. Schendel, and G.R. Patton, "An Empirical Study of Corporate Stagnation and Turnaround," *Proceedings, Academy of Management*, 1975, pp. 49-51.

15. William F. Glueck, *Business Policy: Strategy Formation and Management Action*, 2nd edition (New York, New York: McGraw-Hill Book Company, 1976), pp. 61-71.

16. Francis Joseph Aguilar, *Scanning the Business Environment*, (New York, New York: The MacMillan Company, 1967).

17. Warren Keegan, "Scanning the International Business Environment," unpublished DBA thesis, Harvard Business School, 1967.

18. Robert Collings, "Scanning the Environment for Strategic Information," unpublished DBA thesis, Harvard Business School, 1968.

19. Jerry Wall, "What the Competition is Doing: Your Need To Know," *Harvard Business Review*, November-December, 1974.

20. Ronald Taylor, "Age and Experience as Determinants of Managerial Information Processing and Decisionmaking Performance," *Academy of Management Journal*, Vol. XVIII #1, 1975.

21. William H. Newman, "Strategic Considerations In Planning," *Readings in Management Strategy and Tactics*, Hutchinson, John G., editor, (New York, New York: Holt, Rinehart, and Winston Inc., 1971) pp. 72-79.

22. J. McDonald, *The Game of Business* (Garden City, New York; Doubleday and Company Inc., 1975).

23. Arnold Cooper, E. DeMuzzio, K. Hatten, E. Hicks, and D. Tock, "Strategic Responses to Technological Threats," *Proceeding, Academy of Management*, 1973, pp. 54-60.

24. Peter F. Drucker, *Concept of Corporation*, 2nd edition (New York, New York: The John Day Company, 1972).

25. Peter F. Drucker, *Management: Tasks, Responsibilities, Practices* (New York, New York: Harper & Row Inc., 1973).

26. H. I. Ansoff, R.P. Declerck, and R.L. Hayes, "From Strategic Planning to Strategic Management," *From Strategic Planning To Strategic Management* (New York, New York: Wiley & Sons, Inc., 1976), pp. 39-78.

27. Edwin A. Murray, "Limitations on Strategic Choice," *Proceedings, Academy of Management*, 1976, pp. 140-144.

28. Lawrence R. Jauch, Richard N. Osborn, and William F. Glueck, "Success in Large Business Organizations: The Environment-Strategy Connection," *Proceedings, Academy of Management*, 1977, pp. 113-117.

29. J. Thomas Cannon, *Business Strategy and Policy* (New York, New York: Harcourt, Brace & World Inc., 1968).

30. H.E.R. Uyterhoeven, R.W. Ackerman, and J.W. Rosenblum, *Strategy and Organization: Text and Cases In General Management* (Homewood, Illinois: Richard D. Irwin Inc., 1973).

31. Yudhishter Datta, "Comparative Strategy and Performance of Firms in the U.S. Television Set Industry 1950-1960," unpublished Ph.D. dissertation, State University of New York at Buffalo, 1971.

32. C. Roland Christensen, Kenneth R. Andrews, and Joseph L. Bower, *Business Policy: Text and Cases*, fourth edition (Homewood, Illinois: Richard D. Irwin Inc., 1978).

33. Arthur A. Thompson, and A.J. Strickland, III, *Strategy and Policy: Concepts and Cases* (Dallas, Texas: Business Publications Inc., 1978).

34. Thomas J. McNichols, *Policymaking and Executive Action* (New York, New York: McGraw-Hill Book Company, 1977).

35. Uyterhoeven et al., *Strategy and Organization: Text and Cases In General Management.*

36. Cannon, *Business Strategy and Policy.*

37. William F. Glueck, *Business Policy and Management Action*, 2nd edition (New York, New York: McGraw-Hill, 1976).

38. John Argenti, *Systematic Corporate Planning* (New York, New York: Halstead Press, 1974).

39. Igor H. Ansoff, *Corporate Strategy* (New York, New York: McGraw-Hill Book Company, 1965).

40. Robert L. Katz, *Cases and Concepts in Corporate Strategy* (Englewood Cliffs, New Jersey: Prentice-Hall, Inc., 1970).

41. Michael E. Porter, *Interbrand Choice, Strategy, and Bilateral Market Power* (Cambridge, Massachusetts: Harvard University Press, 1976).

42. George A. Steiner and John B. Miner, *Management Policy and Strategy: Text, Readings, and Cases* (New York, New York: MacMillan Publishing Company, 1977).

43. Edmund P. Learned, et al., *Business Policy: Text and Cases* (Homewood, Illinois: Richard D. Irwin Inc., 1965).

44. Igor H. Ansoff, *Corporate Strategy.*

45. Robert L. Katz, *Cases and Concepts in Corporate Strategy.*

46. Thomas J. Cannon, *Business Strategy and Policy.*

47. George A. Steiner and John B. Miner, *Management Policy and Strategy: Text, Readings, and Cases.*

48. Michael E. Porter, *Interbrand Choice, Strategy, and Bilateral Market Power.*

49. Edmund P. Learned, et al., *Business Policy: Text and Cases.*

50. Thomas J. Cannon, *Business Strategy*, p. XXIV.

51. Edmund P. Learned, et al., *Business Policy*, p. 19.

52. Igor H. Ansoff, *Corporate Strategy*, pp. 111-12.

53. George A. Steiner and John B. Miner, *Management Policy and Strategy: Text, Readings, and Cases*, p. 183.

54. Michael E. Porter, *Interbrand Choice, Strategy, and Bilateral Market Power*, p. 71.

55. Robert L. Katz, *Cases and Concepts in Corporate Strategy.*

56. M.S. Hunt, "Competition In The Major Home Appliance Industry, 1960-1970," Ph.D. dissertation, Business Economics Committee, Harvard University, May 1972.

57. H.H. Newman, "Strategic Groups and the Structure-Performance Relationship: A Study With Respect To The Chemical Process Industries," Ph.D. dissertation, Harvard University, December 1973.

58. Michael E. Porter, *Interbrand Choice, Strategy, and Bilateral Market Power*, p. 76.

59. Endel Jakob Kolde, *The Multinational Company* (Lexington, Massachusetts: Heath and Company, 1974), pp. 26-27.

60. Richard D. Robinson, *International Business Management: A Guide to Decision Making* (New York, New York: Holt, Rinehart, and Winston, Inc., 1973), pp. 14-19.

61. John Snow Schwendiman, *Strategic and Long-Range Planning For The Multinational Corporation* (New York, New York: Praeger Publishers, 1973), pp. 95-99.

62. George A. Steiner and Warren M. Cannon, *Multinational Corporate Planning*, (New York, New York: The MacMillan Co., 1966), pp. 303-4.

63. Endel Jakob Kolde, *The Multinational Company.*

64. Richard D. Robinson, *International Business Management; A Guide to Decision Making.*

65. John Snow Schwendiman, *Strategic and Long-Range Planning For The Multinational Corporation*, pp. 95-99.

66. George A. Steiner and Warren M. Cannon, *Multinational Corporate Planning*, pp. 303-4.

67. Peter F. Drucker, *Management: Tasks, Responsibilities Practices*, (New York, New York: Harper & Row, 1974) pp. 734-36.

68. Robert D. Buzzell "Can You Standardize Multinational Marketing?", *Harvard Business Review*, November-December, 1968, pp. 102-13.

69. Ralph Sorenson and Ulrich Wichman, "How Multinationals View Marketing Standardization," *Harvard Business Review*, May-June 1975, p. 38.

70. Peter F. Drucker, *Management: Tasks, Responsibilities, Practices*, pp. 734-36.

71. Robert D. Buzzell, "Can You Standardize Multinational Marketing?", pp. 102-13.

72. Ralph Sorenson and Ulrich Wichmann, "How Multinationals View Marketing Standardization," p. 38.

73. Endel Jakob Kolde, *International Business Enterprise* (Englewood Cliffs, New Jersey: Prentice-Hall Inc., 1968), pp. 306-11.

74. Michael Z. Brooke and H. Lee Remmers, *The Strategy of Multinational Enterprise* (Great Britain: Longman Group Limited, 1970), pp. 234-38.

75. Stefan H. Robock and Kenneth Simmonds, *International Business and Multinational Enterprises* (Homewood, Illinois: Richard D. Irwin Inc., 1973), pp. 416-8.

76. Richard D. Robinson, *International Management*, (New York, New York: Holt, Rinehart, and Winston, Inc., 1967), pp. 32-44.

77. Michael Z. Brooke, and H. Lee Remmers, *The Strategy of Multinational Enterprise*, pp. 234-238.

78.   Stefan H. Robock and Kenneth Simmonds, *International Business and Multinational Enterprises,* pp. 416-18.

79.   Richard D. Robinson, *International Management,* pp. 32-44.

80.   Ralph Biggadike, *Entering New Markets: Strategies and Performance* (Cambridge, Massachusetts: Marketing Science Institute, 1977).

81.   George S. Day, "A Strategic Perspective On Product Planning," *Journal of Contemporary Business,* Spring, 1975a, pp. 1-35.

82.   Gorden E. Miracle and Gerald S. Albaum, *International Marketing Management* (Homewood, Illinois, Richard D. Irwin Inc., 1970), pp. 278-305.

83.   Warren J. Keegan, "Multinational Product Planning: Strategic Alternatives," *Journal of Marketing,* Vol. 33, January 1969, pp. 58-62.

84.   Michael Z. Brooke, and H. Lee Remmers, *The Strategy of Multinational Enterprise,* pp. 234-38.

85.   Richard D. Robinson, *International Business Management: A Guide To Decision Making,* pp. 14-19.

86.   Richard D. Robinson, *International Management,* pp. 32-44.

87.   Stefan H. Robock and Kenneth Simmonds, *International Business and Multinational Enterprises,* pp. 416-18.

88.   John Snow Schwendiman, *Strategic and Long-Range Planning For The Multinational Corporation,* pp. 95-99.

89.   George A. Steiner and Warren M. Cannon, *Multinational Corporate Planning,* pp. 303-4.

90.   H. Igor Ansoff, *Corporate Strategy.*

91.   Endel Jakob Kolde, *The Multinational Company,* pp. 26-27.

92.   Robert F. Lanzillotti, "Multiple Products and Oligopoly Strategy: A Development of Chamberlin's Theory of Products," *Quarterly Journal of Economics,* August, 1954, pp. 461-74.

93.   Theodore Levitt, "Improving Sales Through Product Augmentation," *European Business,* April, 1969, pp. 5-12.

94.   Spencer Klaw, "The Soap Wars: A Strategic Analysis," *Fortune,* June, 1963, pp. 123+.

95. Sidney Schoeffler, Robert D. Buzzell, and Donald F. Heany, "Impact of Strategic Planning on Profit Performance," *Harvard Business Review*, March-April, 1974, pp. 137-45.

96. Bradley T. Gale, "Market Share and Rate of Return," *Review of Economics and Statistics*, November, 1972, pp. 412-23.

97. Robert D. Buzzell, Bradley T. Gale, and Ralph G.M. Sultan, "Market Share: A Key to Profitability," *Harvard Business Review*, January-February, 1975, pp. 97-106.

98. Boston Consulting Group – Staff, *Perspectives On Experience*, Boston Consulting Group, Boston, Massachusetts, 1968.

99. Sidney Schoeffler, Robert D. Buzzell, and Donald F. Heany, "Impact of Strategic Planning On Profit Performance," pp. 137-45.

100. Robert D. Buzzell, Bradley T. Gale, and Ralph G.M. Sultan, "Market Share: A Key to Profitability," pp. 97-106.

101. Boston Consulting Group – Staff, *Perspectives On Experience*.

102. J.A. Menge, "Style Change Costs as a Market Weapon", *Quarterly Journal of Economics*, November, 1962, pp. 215-32.

103. John S. McGee, "Economies of Size In Auto Body Manufacturing," *Journal of Law and Economics*, Vol. XVI, October, 1973.

104. Lawrence Jay White, *The American Automobile Industry in the Postwar Period*, Ph.D. dissertation, Department of Economics, Harvard University, 1969.

105. D.G. Rhys, *The Motor Industry: An Economic Survey*, (London, Butterworth's Ltd., 1972).

106. James C. Abegglen, "Perspectives: Japan's Economy and the Foreign Company," Boston Consulting Group, Boston, Mass., 1976.

107. James C. Abegglen, "Perspectives: The Foreign Company in Japan – 1977," Boston Consulting Group, Boston, Mass., 1977.

108. Sanford Rose, "The Secret of Japan's Export Prowess," *Fortune*, January 30, 1978, pp. 56-63.

109. James C. Abegglen, "Perspectives: Japan's Economy and the Foreign Company."

110. James C. Abegglen, "Perspectives: The Foreign Company in Japan – 1977."

111. Sanford Rose, "The Secret of Japan's Export Prowess," pp. 56-63.

112. George S. Day, "A Strategic Perspective On Product Planning," pp. 1-35.

113. Ralph Biggadike, *Entering New Markets: Strategies and Performance.*

114. George S. Day, "A Strategic Perspective On Product Planning," pp. 1-35.

115. Ralph Biggadike, *Entering New Markets: Strategies and Performance.*

116. Bernard Catry, and Michel Chevalier, "Market Share Strategy and the Product Life Cycle," *Journal of Marketing,* October, 1974, pp. 29-34.

117. Yoram Wind, and Henry J. Claycamp, "Planning Product Line Strategy: A Matrix Approach," *Journal of Marketing,* January, 1976, pp. 2-9.

118. George S. Day, "Diagnosing the Product Portfolio," *Journal of Marketing,* April, 1977, pp. 29-38.

119. Bernard Catry, and Michel Chevalier, "Market Share Strategy and the Product Life Cycle," pp. 29-34.

120. Yoram Wind, and Henry J. Claycamp, "Planning Product Line Strategy: A Matrix Approach," pp. 2-9.

121. George S. Day, "Diagnosing the Product Portfolio," pp. 29-34.

122. Robert D. Buzzell, Bradley T. Gale, and Ralph G.M. Sultan, "Market Share: A Key to Profitability," pp. 97-106.

123. Paul N. Bloom and Philip Kotler, "Strategies For High Market Share Companies," *Harvard Business Review,* November-December, 1975, pp. 63-72.

124. Walter J. Talley, "Profiting From the Declining Product," *Business Horizons,* Spring, 1964, pp. 77-84.

125. Philip Kotler, "Phasing Out Weak Products," *Harvard Business Review,* March-April, 1965, pp. 107-18.

126. Robert D. Buzzell, Bradley T. Gale, and Ralph G.M. Sultan, "Market Share: A Key to Profitability," pp. 97-106.

127. Paul N. Bloom and Philip Kotler, "Strategies For High Market Share Companies," pp. 63-72.

128. Robert F. Lanzillotti, "Multiple Products and Oligopoly Strategy: A Development of Chamberlin's Theory of Products," pp. 461-74.

129. William J. Abernathy, and Kenneth Wayne, "Limits of the Learning Curve," *Harvard Business Review*, September-October, 1974, pp. 109-19.

130. William E. Fruhan, "Pyrrhic Victories in Fights For Market Share," *Harvard Business Review*, Sept.-Oct. 1972, pp. 100-107.

131. Seymour Tilles, "How To Evaluate Corporate Strategy," *Harvard Business Review*, July-August, 1963, pp. 111-21.

132. Theodore Levitt, "Marketing Myopia," *Harvard Business Review*, July-August, 1960.

133. Paul N. Bloom and Philip Kotler, "Strategies For High Market Share Companies," pp. 63-72.

134. William E. Fruhan, "Pyrrhic Victories In Fights For Market Share," pp. 100-107.

135. Theodore Levitt, "Marketing Myopia."

CHAPTER 3

1. Ronald E. Frank and Paul E. Green, "Numerical Taxonomy In Marketing Analysis: A Review Article," *Journal of Marketing Research*, February 1968, pp. 83-98.

2. Ronald E. Frank, William F. Massy, and Yoram Wind, *Market Segmentation* (Englewood Cliffs, New Jersey: Prentice-Hall, 1972), pp. 202-5.

3. Paul E. Green, and Yoram Wind, *Multiattribute Decisions In Marketing: A Measurement Approach* (Hinsdale, Illinois: The Dryden Press, 1973), pp. 369-71.

4. John A. Hartigan, *Clustering Algorithms* (New York, New York: John Wiley and Sons, 1975), pp. 89-91.

5. George S. Day, and Allan Shocker, *Identifying Competitive Product-Market Boundaries: Strategic and Analytical Issues* (Cambridge, Massachusetts: Marketing Science Institute, 1976).

6. Herman E. Krooss and Charles Gilbert, *American Business History* (Englewood Cliffs, New Jersey: Prentice Hall, 1972), p. 307.

7. Alfred D. Chandler, Jr., editor, *Giant Enterprise*, (New York, New York: Harcourt, Brace and World, 1964).

8. William H. Reynolds, "The Edsel, Ten Years Later," *Business Horizons*, Fall 1967, pp. 39-46.

9. Herman E. Krooss and Charles Gilbert, *American Business History*, pp. 308-15.

10. Alfred D. Chandler and Stephen Salsbury, *Pierre S. DuPont and The Making of the Modern Corporation* (New York, New York: Harper and Row, 1971), pp. 537-559.

CHAPTER 4

1. Paul E. Green, and Carroll, J. Douglas, *Mathematical Tools for Applied Multivariate Analysis* (New York, New York: Academic Press, 1976), pp. 282-84.

2. Ben W. Bolch, and Huang, Cliff J., *Multivariate Statistical Methods For Business and Economics* (Englewood Cliffs, New Jersey: Prentice-Hall Inc., 1974), pp. 90-93 and 232-38.

3. William W. Cooley, and Lohnes, Paul R., *Multivariate Data Analysis* (New York, New York: John Wiley & Sons Inc., 1971), pp. 226-30.

4. Maurice M. Tatsuoka, *Multivariate Analysis* (New York, New York: John Wiley & Sons Inc., 1971), pp. 164-170.

5. Maurice M. Tatsuoka, "Discriminant Analysis," pamphlet, Institute For Personality and Ability Testing, Champaign, Illinois, 1970, pp. 48-51.

6. Paul E. Green, and Tull, Donald S., *Research For Marketing Decisions*, fourth edition, (Englewood Cliffs, New Jersey: 1978), pp. 393-94.

7. Maurice M. Tatsuoka, "Discriminant Analysis," p. 48.

8. William Lee Hays, *Statistics* (New York, New York: Holt, Rinehart, and Winston, 1963).

9. Paul E. Green, et al., *Research For Marketing Decisions*, p. 394.

10. Norman H. Nie, Hull, C. Hadlai, Jenkins, Jean G., Steinbrenner, Karin, and Brent, Dale H., *Statistical Package For The Social Sciences — 2nd Edition* (New York, New York: 1975), pp. 434-67.

CHAPTER 6

1. James C. Abegglen, "Perspectives: Japan's Economy and the Foreign Company," Boston Consulting Group, Boston, Massachusetts, 1976.

2. James C. Abegglen, "Perspectives: The Foreign Company in Japan — 1977," Boston Consulting Group, Boston, Massachusetts, 1977.

3. Sanford Rose, "The Secret of Japan's Export Prowess," *Fortune*, January 30, 1978, pp. 56-63.

4.   Gene Bylinski, "The Japanese Spies In Silicon Valley," *Fortune*, February 27, 1978, pp. 74-81.

CHAPTER 7

1.   Robert N. Anthony, John Dearden, and Richard F. Vancil, *Management Control Systems: Text, Cases, and Readings* (Homewood, Illinois: Richard D. Irwin, Inc., 1972), pp. 104-107.

2.   Philip Kotler, *Marketing Management: Analysis, Planning, and Control*, p. 360.

3.   Edmund P. Learned, Charles R. Christensen, and Kenneth R. Andrews, *Problems of General Management — Business Policy* (Homewood, Illinois: Richard D. Irwin, Inc., 1961), p. 88.

4.   Seymour Tilles, "How To Evaluate Corporate Strategy," pp. 111-21.

5.   Robert L. Katz, *Cases and Concepts in Corporate Strategy*, p. 205.

6.   Norman H. Nie, C. Hadlai Hull, Jean G. Jenkins, Karin Steinbrenner, and Dale H. Bent, *Statistical Package For The Social Sciences — 2nd Edition*, pp. 434-467.

7.   Ibid.

CHAPTER 8

1.   M.S. Hunt, "Competition In The Major Home Appliance Industry, 1960-1970."

2.   H.H. Newman, "Strategic Groups and the Structure-Performance Relationship: A Study With Respect To The Chemical Process Industries."

3.   Michael E. Porter, *Interbrand Choice, Strategy, and Bilateral Market Power.*

4.   John A. Hartigan, *Clustering Algorithms*, (New York, New York: John Wiley and Sons, 1975), pp. 89-91.

CHAPTER 10

1.   *Statistical Abstract of the United States 1976*, p. 593.

2.   Ibid.

3.   "The Fortune Directory of the 500 Largest U.S. Industrial Corporations," p. 366.

4.   *Statistical Abstract of the United States 1976*, p. 378.

5.   Ibid.

6.   George S. Day and Allan Shocker, *Identifying Competitive Product-Market Boundaries: Strategic and Analytical Issues.*

7.   James C. Abegglen, "Perspectives: Japan's Economy and the Foreign Company."

8.   James C. Abegglen, "Perspectives: The Foreign Company In Japan — 1977."

9.   Sanford Rose, "The Secret of Japan's Export Prowess."

10.   Gene Bylinski, "The Japanese Spies In Silicon Valley," pp. 74-81.

11.   M.S. Hunt, "Competition In The Major Home Appliance Industry, 1960-1970."

12.   H.H. Newman, "Strategic Groups and the Structure-Performance Relationship: A Study With Respect To The Chemical Process Industries."

13.   Michael·E. Porter, *Interbrand Choice, Strategy, and Bilateral Market Power.*

14.   Ralph Biggadike, *Entering New Markets: Strategies and Performance.*

15.   John Snow Schwendiman, *Strategic and Long-Range Planning For The Multinational Corporation.*

Appendix A

Correlations Among the Strategic Dimensions

Table A-1

Within Groups Correlations Between the Dimensions of the Group of Strategic Profile Vectors for Volkswagen and for the Other German and Japanese Automanufacturers

Within Groups Correlation Matrix					
	No. of Models	No. of Product Groups	No. of Dealers	Price of Most Popular Model	Estimated Advertising
Number of Models	1.00000				
Number of Product Groups	.67269	1.00000			
Number of Dealers	.35300	.16610	1.00000		
Price of Most Popular Model	.13919	.44694	-.36827	1.00000	
Estimated Advertising	.54169	.38554	.64890	-.32948	1.00000

Table A-2

Within Groups Correlations Between the Dimensions of the Group of Strategic Changes Vectors for Volkswagen and for the Other German and Japanese Automanufacturers

	Within Groups Correlation Matrix				
	No. of Models	No. of Product Groups	No. of Dealers	Price of Most Popular Model	Estimated Advertising
Number of Models	1.00000				
Number of Product Groups	.20186	1.00000			
Number of Dealers	-.14096	-.30013	1.00000		
Price of Most Popular Model	-34633	-.12849	.17878	1.00000	
Estimated Advertising	-.32604	-.28102	.40169	.13833	1.00000

Table A-3

Within Groups Correlations Between the Dimensions of the Group of Strategic Profile Vectors for the German and for the Japanese Automanufacturers

	Within Groups Correlation Matrix				
	No. of Models	No. of Product Groups	No. of Dealers	Price of Most Popular Model	Estimated Advertising
Number of Models	1.00000				
Number of Product Groups	.69847	1.00000			
Number of Dealers	.29014	.15471	1.00000		
Price of Most Popular Model	.16285	.37235	-.35645	1.00000	
Estimated Advertising	.42010	.26566	.79672	-.43149	1.00000

Table A-4

Within Groups Correlations Between the Dimensions of the Group of Strategic Changes Vectors for the German and for the Japanese Automanufacturers

	Within Groups Correlation Matrix				
	No. of Models	No. of Product Groups	No. of Dealers	Price of Most Popular Model	Estimated Advertising
Number of Models	1.00000				
Number of Product Groups	.16927	1.00000			
Number of Dealers	-.19296	-.33423	1.00000		
Price of Most Popular Model	-.39098	.12534	.14940	1.00000	
Estimated Advertising	-.31774	-.28329	.42738	.13207	1.00000

Table A-5

Within Groups Correlations Between the Dimensions of the Group of Strategic Profile Vectors for the Higher Volume and for the Lower Volume Automanufacturers

	No. of Models	No. of Product Groups	No. of Dealers	Price of Most Popular Model	Estimated Advertising
			Within Groups Correlation Matrix		
Number of Models	1.00000				
Number of Product Groups	.63778	1.00000			
Number of Dealers	-.24010	-.38194	1.00000		
Price of Most Popular Model	.36098	.63184	-.12648	1.00000	
Estimated Advertising	.13946	.03954	.09290	-.08421	1.00000

Table A-6

Within Groups Correlations Between the Dimensions of the Group of Strategic Changes Vectors for the Higher Volume and for the Lower Volume Automanufacturers

	Within Groups Correlation Matrix				
	No. of Models	No. of Product Groups	No. of Dealers	Price of Most Popular Model	Estimated Advertising
Number of Models	1.00000				
Number of Product Groups	.19017	1.00000			
Number of Dealers	-.09805	-.23950	1.00000		
Price of Most Popular Model	-.35187	-.12387	.16154	1.00000	
Estimated Advertising	-.31239	-.24882	.36381	.13184	1.00000

Table A-7

Pearson Product Moment Correlations
Between the Dimensions
of the Strategic Profile Vectors of All of the Firms

	No. of Models	No. of P/M Groups	No. of Dealers	Price	Advertising
Number of Models	1.0	.6703*	.2837**	.1354	.4200*
Number of Product/ Market Groups	.6703*	1.0	.0853	.4519*	.2469**
Number of Dealers	.2837**	.0853	1.0	-.4087*	.7841*
Price of Most Popular Model	.1354	.4519*	-.4087*	1.0	-.3766*
Advertising	.4200*	.2469**	.7841*	-.3766*	1.0

* = correlation coefficient significant at the .99 level.
** = correlation coefficient significant at the .94 level.

Table A-8

Pearson Product Moment Correlations
Between the Dimensions
of the Japanese Firms' Strategic Profile Vectors

	No. of Models	No. of P/M Groups	No. of Dealers	Price	Advertising
Number of Models	1.0	.7995*	.5064*	.2026	.6748*
Number of Product/ Market Groups	.7995*	1.0	.5366*	.1469	.6569*
Number of Dealers	.5064*	.5366*	1.0	-.0354	.6081*
Price of Most Popular Model	.2026	.1469	-.0354	1.0	.0122
Advertising	.6748*	.6569*	.6081*	.0122	1.0

* = correlation coefficient significant at the .99 level.

Table A-9

Pearson Product Moment Correlations
Between the Dimensions
of the German Firms' Strategic Profile Vectors

	No. of Models	No. of P/M Groups	No. of Dealers	Price	Advertising
Number of Models	1.0	.4681**	.0485	.2435	.0935
Number of Product/ Market Groups	.4681**	1.0	-.2621	.6126*	-.2093
Number of Dealers	.0485	-.2621	1.0	-.4623**	.9324*
Price of Most Popular Model	.2435	.6126*	-.4623**	1.0	-.5965*
Advertising	.0935	-.2093	.9324*	-.5965*	1.0

* = correlation coefficient significant at the .99 level.
** = correlation coefficient significant at the .98 level.

Table A-10

Pearson Product Moment Correlations Between the Dimensions of the Japanese Firms' Strategic Changes Vectors

	No. of Models	No. of P/M Groups	No. of Dealers	Price	Advertising
Number of Models	1.0	.1595	-.1064	-.5175*	-.3409**
Number of Product/ Market Groups	.1595	1.0	-.3893**	-.1990	-.5054**
Number of Dealers	-.1064	-.3893**	1.0	.1871	.5405*
Price of Most Popular Model	-.5175	-.1990	.1871	1.0	.3238**
Advertising	-.3409**	-.5054**	.5405*	.3238**	1.0

*   = correlation coefficient significant at the .99 level.
** = correlation coefficient significant at the .90 level.

Table A-11

Pearson Product Moment Correlations Between the Dimensions of the German Firms' Strategic Changes Vectors

	No. of Models	No. of P/M Groups	No. of Dealers	Price	Advertising
Number of Models	1.0	.2107	-.5728*	-.1135	-.3640**
Number of Product Market Groups	.2107	1.0	-.1007	.0430	.0206
Number of Dealers	-.5728*	-.1007	1.0	.0701	.3474**
Price of Most Popular Model	-.1135	.0430	.0701	1.0	-.0570
Advertising	-.3640**	.0206	.3474**	-.0570	1.0

* = correlation coefficient significant at the .99 level.
** = correlation coefficient significant at the .90 level.

Table A-12

Pearson Product Moment Correlations Between the Dimensions of the Higher Volume Firms' Strategic Profile Vectors

	No. of Models	No. of P/M Groups	No. of Dealers	Price	Advertising
Number of Models	1.0	.4490*	-.3931**	-.0532	-.3416
Number of Product/ Market Groups	.4490*	1.0	-.4614*	.5293*	-.5794*
Number of Dealers	-.3931**	-.4614*	1.0	-.0640	.5416*
Price of Most Popular Model	-.0532	.5293*	-.0640	1.0	-.0315
Advertising	-.3416	-.5794*	.5416*	-.0315	1.0

* = correlation coefficient significant at the .95 level.
** = correlation coefficient significant at the .90 level.

Table A-13

Pearson Product Moment Correlations Between the Dimensions of the Lower Volume Firms' Strategic Profile Vectors

	No. of Models	No. of P/M Groups	No. of Dealers	Price	Advertising
Number of Models	1.0	.6816*	-.2025	.4065**	.3737**
Number of Product/ Market Groups	.6816*	1.0	-.3628**	.6767*	.3261**
Number of Dealers	-.2025	-.3628**	1.0	-.1391	.1188
Price of Most Popular Model	.4065**	.6767*	-.1391	1.0	-.1140
Advertising	.3737**	.3261**	-.1188	-.1140	1.0

* = correlation coefficient significant at the .99 level.
** = correlation coefficient significant at the .95 level.

Table A-14

Pearson Product Moment Correlations Between the Dimensions
of the Strategic Changes Vectors of the Higher Volume Firms

	No. of Models	No. of P/M Groups	No. of Dealers	Price	Advertising
Number of Models	1.0	.2453	.2906	-.4608*	.2746
Number of Product/ Market Groups	.2453	1.0	-.0066	.2505	-.4504*
Number of Dealers	.2906	-.0066	1.0	-.2246	-.3450
Price of Most Popular Model	-.4608*	.2505	-.2246	1.0	-.2086
Advertising	.2746	-.4504*	-.3450	-.2086	1.0

* = correlation coefficient significant at the .90 level.

Table A-15

Pearson Product Moment Correlations Between the Dimensions of the Strategic Changes Vectors of the Lower Volume Firms

	No. of Models	No. of P/M Groups	No. of Dealers	Price	Advertising
Number of Models	1.0	.2001	-.1190	-.3361**	-.3658*
Number of Product/ Market Groups	.2001	1.0	-.3458*	-.3058**	-.2524
Number of Dealers	-.1190	-.3458*	1.0	.1911	.3901*
Price of Most Popular Model	-.3361**	-.3058**	-.1911	1.0	.1707
Advertising	-.3658*	-.2524	.3901*	.1707	1.0

* = correlation coefficient significant at the .95 level.
** = correlation coefficient significant at the .90 level.

Appendix B

Product/Market Groups and Identification of Direct Competitors by Years

Table B-1

Number of Models by Segment by Year

1965	6 Segments						1966	5 Segments				
	1	2	3	4	5	6		1	2	3	4	5
VW	-	-	-	-	2	-	VW	-	-	-	-	4
BMW	-	-	1	-	-	-	BMW	-	2	-	-	-
MB	-	1	3	1	-	3	MB	-	4	1	2	-
PA	6	-	-	-	-	-	PA	4	-	-	1	2
TY	-	-	2	1	1	-	TY	-	2	-	1	1
NI	-	-	1	1	3	-	NI	-	-	-	1	3

1967	6 Segments						1968	6 Segments					
	1	2	3	4	5	6		1	2	3	4	5	6
VW	-	-	-	-	-	4	VW	-	-	-	-	4	-
BMW	-	-	-	2	-	1	BMW	-	-	-	-	2	-
MB	-	1	1	5	3	-	MB	-	1	1	4	-	3
PA	5	2	-	-	-	2	PA	5	2	-	1	3	-
TY	-	1	-	2	-	1	TY	-	1	-	2	2	1
NI	-	1	-	-	-	5	NI	-	1	-	-	3	-
HN	-	-	-	-	-	-	HN	1	-	-	-	-	-

1969	9 Segments								
	1	2	3	4	5	6	7	8	9
VW	-	-	-	-	4	-	-	-	-
BMW	-	1	-	-	-	-	-	2	2
MB	-	3	1	1	-	1	-	-	4
PA	-	-	-	1	2	-	-	2	-
TY	-	2	-	-	1	-	2	2	-
TK	-	-	-	-	-	-	-	-	-
NI	-	-	-	-	-	-	-	5	-
HN	1	-	-	-	-	-	-	-	-
SU	1	-	-	-	-	-	-	-	-

Table B-1 (continued)

1970	8 Segments							
	1	2	3	4	5	6	7	8
VW	-	-	-	-	2	-	2	-
BMW	-	-	-	-	2	3	-	-
MB	-	1	1	3	-	5	-	1
PA	-	3	-	-	5	-	3	2
TY	-	-	-	-	5	-	3	2
TK	-	-	-	-	-	-	-	-
NI	-	1	-	-	5	-	-	-
HN	1	-	-	-	-	-	-	-
SU	1	-	-	-	-	-	2	-

1971	7 Segments						
	1	2	3	4	5	6	7
VW	3	-	-	-	5	-	-
BMW	-	-	-	-	2	-	4
MB	-	2	1	3	-	-	5
PA	3	2	-	-	5	3	-
TY	3	2	-	-	9	-	-
TK	3	-	-	-	5	-	-
NI	2	-	-	-	3	2	-
HN	1	-	-	-	-	-	-
SU	3	-	-	-	-	-	-

1972	12 Segments											
	1	2	3	4	5	6	7	8	9	10	11	12
VW	-	-	-	-	-	-	-	3	-	5	-	-
BMW	-	-	-	-	-	2	-	-	2	-	-	-
MB	-	-	1	-	-	3	2	-	-	-	3	2
PA	-	-	3	-	6	-	-	-	4	-	-	-
TY	-	-	-	4	-	-	-	-	5	-	-	-
TK	-	-	-	7	-	-	-	-	4	1	-	-
NI	-	1	-	2	-	-	-	-	3	-	-	-
HN	2	-	-	-	-	-	-	-	-	-	-	-
SU	-	-	-	-	-	-	3	-	-	-	-	-

1973	16 Segments															
	1	2	3	4	5	6	7	8	9	10	11	12	13	14	15	16
VW	-	-	-	-	-	-	-	-	-	-	-	-	3	-	-	5
BMW	-	-	-	-	-	-	-	-	-	2	-	-	-	-	3	-
MB	-	1	-	-	-	3	-	-	2	-	2	-	-	-	-	-
PA	-	-	2	4	-	-	-	-	-	-	-	-	-	3	-	-
TY	-	-	5	-	-	-	1	3	-	-	-	3	-	-	-	-
TK	-	-	-	-	-	-	-	6	-	2	-	-	-	-	-	-
NI	-	-	1	-	1	-	2	-	-	3	-	-	-	-	-	-
HN	-	-	-	-	-	-	1	-	-	-	-	-	-	-	-	-
SU	4	-	-	-	-	-	-	-	-	-	-	-	-	-	-	-

Table B-1 (continued)

| 1974 | 14 Segments |

	1	2	3	4	5	6	7	8	9	10	11	12	13	14
VW	-	-	-	3	-	-	-	-	1	-	-	-	4	-
BMW	-	-	-	-	-	-	2	-	-	-	3	-	-	-
MB	-	2	-	-	3	-	-	1	-	-	-	-	-	2
PA	-	-	-	3	-	-	-	-	-	1	-	3	-	-
TY	-	-	-	-	-	4	6	-	-	3	-	-	-	-
TK	-	-	-	-	-	1	3	-	2	2	-	-	-	-
NI	-	-	1	-	-	3	6	-	-	-	-	-	-	-
HN	-	-	-	-	-	1	-	-	-	-	-	-	-	-
SU	4	-	-	-	-	-	-	-	-	-	-	-	-	-

| 1975 | 12 Segments |

	1	2	3	4	5	6	7	8	9	10	11	12
VW	-	-	1	-	-	-	5	-	-	-	-	-
BMW	-	2	-	-	-	-	-	1	-	-	-	-
MB	-	-	-	3	-	3	-	-	3	-	-	1
PA	-	-	1	-	2	-	2	1	-	-	-	-
TY	-	-	6	-	-	-	-	3	-	3	-	-
TK	-	-	-	-	-	-	-	3	-	4	-	-
NI	-	-	6	-	1	-	-	-	-	2	1	-
HN	2	-	-	-	-	-	-	-	-	-	-	-
SU	-	-	-	-	-	-	5	-	-	-	-	-

| 1976 | 13 Segments |

	1	2	3	4	5	6	7	8	9	10	11	12	13
VW	-	-	-	-	-	1	-	4	-	-	-	1	-
BMW	-	-	-	-	2	-	-	-	-	-	-	1	-
MB	-	-	-	3	1	-	3	-	-	-	-	-	3
PA	-	1	1	-	-	1	-	1	-	1	-	-	-
TY	-	-	-	-	-	-	-	3	1	2	1	5	-
TK	6	-	-	-	-	2	-	-	-	4	-	-	-
NI	2	-	1	-	-	-	-	-	1	-	-	6	-
HN	3	-	-	-	-	-	-	-	-	-	-	-	-
SU	-	-	-	-	-	-	-	6	-	-	-	-	-

Penetrating the U. S. Auto Market

Table B-2

Companies Competing in the Same Market Segments

		VW	BMW	MB	PA	TY	TK	NI	HN	SU	
VW	65	X	N	N	N	Y	X	Y	X	X	
	66	X	N	N	Y	Y	X	Y	X	X	
	67	X	Y	N	Y	Y	X	Y	X	X	
	68	X	Y	N	Y	Y	X	Y	N	X	X = no models in
	69	X	N	N	Y	Y	X	N	N	N	U.S. market
	70	X	Y	N	Y	Y	X	Y	N	Y	
	71	X	Y	N	Y	Y	Y	Y	Y	Y	N = did not
	72	X	N	N	N	N	Y	N	N	Y	compete
	73	X	N	N	N	N	N	N	N	N	
	74	X	N	N	Y	N	Y	N	N	N	Y = competed
	75	X	N	N	Y	Y	N	Y	N	Y	
	76	X	Y	N	Y	Y	Y	Y	N	Y	
BMW	65	N	X	Y	N	Y	X	Y	X	X	
	66	N	X	Y	N	Y	X	N	X	X	
	67	Y	X	Y	Y	N	X	Y	X	X	
	68	Y	X	N	Y	N	X	Y	N	X	
	69	N	X	Y	Y	Y	X	Y	N	N	
	70	Y	X	Y	Y	Y	X	Y	N	N	
	71	Y	X	Y	Y	Y	Y	Y	N	N	
	72	N	X	Y	Y	Y	Y	Y	N	N	
	73	N	X	N	N	N	Y	Y	N	N	
	74	Y	X	N	N	Y	Y	Y	N	N	
	75	N	X	N	Y	Y	Y	N	N	N	
	76	Y	X	Y	N	Y	N	Y	N	N	
MB	65	N	Y	X	N	Y	X	Y	X	X	
	66	N	Y	X	Y	Y	X	Y	X	X	
	67	N	Y	X	Y	Y	X	Y	X	X	
	68	N	N	X	Y	Y	X	Y	N	X	
	69	N	Y	X	Y	Y	X	N	N	N	
	70	N	Y	X	Y	Y	X	Y	N	N	
	71	N	Y	X	Y	Y	N	N	N	N	
	72	N	Y	X	Y	N	N	N	N	N	
	73	N	N	X	N	N	N	N	N	N	
	74	N	N	X	N	N	N	N	N	N	
	75	N	N	X	N	N	N	N	N	N	
	76	N	Y	X	N	N	N	N	N	N	
PA	65	N	N	N	X	N	X	N	X	X	
	66	Y	N	Y	X	Y	X	Y	X	X	
	67	Y	Y	Y	X	Y	X	Y	X	X	
	68	Y	Y	Y	X	Y	X	Y	Y	X	
	69	Y	Y	Y	X	Y	X	Y	N	N	
	70	Y	Y	Y	X	Y	X	Y	N	Y	
	71	Y	Y	Y	X	Y	Y	Y	Y	Y	
	72	N	Y	Y	X	Y	Y	Y	N	N	
	73	N	N	N	X	Y	N	Y	N	N	
	74	Y	N	N	X	Y	Y	N	N	N	
	75	Y	Y	N	X	Y	Y	Y	N	Y	
	76	Y	N	N	X	Y	Y	Y	N	Y	

Table B-2 (Continued)

		VW	BMW	MB	PA	TY	TK	NI	HN	SU
TY	65	Y	Y	Y	N	X	X	Y	X	X
	66	Y	Y	Y	Y	X	X	Y	X	X
	67	Y	N	Y	Y	X	X	Y	X	X
	68	Y	N	Y	Y	X	X	Y	N	X
	69	Y	Y	Y	Y	X	X	Y	N	N
	70	Y	Y	Y	Y	X	X	Y	N	Y
	71	Y	Y	Y	Y	X	Y	Y	Y	Y
	72	N	Y	N	Y	X	Y	Y	N	N
	73	N	N	N	Y	X	Y	Y	Y	N
	74	N	Y	N	Y	X	Y	Y	Y	N
	75	Y	Y	N	Y	X	Y	Y	N	N
	76	Y	Y	N	Y	X	Y	Y	N	Y
TK	71	Y	Y	N	Y	Y	X	Y	Y	Y
	72	Y	Y	N	Y	Y	X	Y	N	N
	73	N	Y	N	N	Y	X	Y	N	N
	74	Y	Y	N	Y	Y	X	Y	Y	N
	75	N	Y	N	Y	Y	X	Y	N	N
	76	Y	N	N	Y	Y	X	Y	Y	N
NI	65	Y	Y	Y	N	Y	X	X	X	X
	66	Y	N	Y	Y	Y	X	X	X	X
	67	Y	Y	Y	Y	Y	X	X	X	X
	68	Y	Y	Y	Y	Y	X	X	N	X
	69	N	Y	N	Y	Y	X	X	N	N
	70	Y	Y	Y	Y	Y	X	X	N	N
	71	Y	Y	N	Y	Y	Y	X	Y	Y
	72	N	Y	N	Y	Y	Y	X	N	N
	73	N	Y	N	Y	Y	Y	X	Y	N
	74	N	Y	N	N	Y	Y	X	Y	N
	75	Y	N	N	Y	Y	Y	X	N	N
	76	Y	Y	N	Y	Y	Y	X	Y	N
HN	68	N	N	N	Y	N	X	N	X	X
	69	N	N	N	N	N	X	N	X	Y
	70	N	N	N	N	N	X	N	X	Y
	71	Y	N	N	Y	Y	Y	Y	X	Y
	72	N	N	N	N	N	N	N	X	N
	73	N	N	N	N	Y	N	Y	X	N
	74	N	N	N	N	Y	Y	Y	X	N
	75	N	N	N	N	N	N	N	X	N
	76	N	N	N	N	N	Y	Y	X	N
SU	69	N	N	N	N	N	X	N	Y	X
	70	Y	N	N	Y	Y	X	N	Y	X
	71	Y	N	N	Y	Y	Y	Y	Y	X
	72	Y	N	N	N	N	N	N	N	X
	73	N	N	N	N	N	N	N	N	X
	74	N	N	N	N	N	N	N	N	X
	75	Y	N	N	Y	N	N	N	N	X
	76	Y	N	N	Y	Y	N	N	N	X

Bibliography

BOOKS

Aguilar, Francis Joseph. *Scanning the Business Environment.* New York, New York: The MacMillan Company, 1967.

Ansoff, H. Igor. *Corporate Strategy.* New York, New York: McGraw-Hill Book Company, 1965.

Anthony, Robert N.; Dearden, John; and Vancil, Richard F. *Management Control Systems: Text, Cases, and Readings.* Homewood, Illinois: Richard D. Irwin Inc., 1972.

Argenti, John. *Systematic Corporate Planning.* New York, New York: Halstead Press, 1974.

Biggadike, Ralph. *Entering New Markets: Strategies and Performance.* Cambridge, Massachusetts: Marketing Science Institute, 1977.

Bolch, Ben W.; and Huang, Cliff J. *Multivariate Statistical Methods For Business and Economics.* Englewood Cliffs, New Jersey: Prentice-Hall Inc., 1974.

Boston Consulting Group – Staff. *Perspectives On Experience.* Boston, Massachusetts: Boston Consulting Group, 1968.

Brooke, Michael Z.; and Remmers, H. Lee. *The Strategy of Multinational Enterprise.* Great Britain: Longman Group Limited, 1970.

Cannon, J. Thomas. *Business Strategy and Policy.* New York, New York; Harcourt, Brace & World Inc. 1968.

Chandler, Alfred D. Jr., editor. *Giant Enterprise.* New York, New York: Harcourt, Brace and World, 1964.

_____; and Salsbury, Stephen. *Pierre S. DuPont and the Making of the Modern Corporation.* New York, New York: Harper & Row Inc., 1971.

Chandler, Alfred D. Jr., editor. *Strategy and Structure: Chapters in the History of American Industrial Enterprise.* Cambridge, Mass.: The M.I.T. Press, 1962.

Chow, Gregory C. *Demand For Automobiles In The United States: A Study In Consumer Durables.* Amsterdam, The Netherlands: North Holland Publishing Company, 1957.

Christensen, C. Roland; Andrews, Kenneth R.; and Bower, Joseph L. *Business Policy: Text and Cases.* Fourth Edition. Homewood, Illinois: Richard D. Irwin Inc., 1978.

Cooley, William W.; and Lohnes, Paul R. *Multivariate Data Analysis.* New York, New York: John Wiley & Sons, Inc., 1971.

Day, George S.; and Shocker, Allan. *Identifying Competitive Product-Market Boundaries: Strategic and Analytical Issues.* Cambridge, Massachusetts: Marketing Science Institute, 1976.

Drucker, Peter F. *Concept of the Corporation.* Second Edition. New York, New York: The John Day Company, 1972.

_____. *Management: Tasks, Responsibilities, Practices.* New York, New York: Harper & Row, 1974.

Fisher, Sir Ronald Aylmer. *Statistical Methods For Research Workers.* Darien, Connecticut: Hafner Publishing Company, 1970.

Frank, Ronald, E.; Massy, William F.; and Wind, Yoram. *Market Segmentation.* Englewood Cliffs, New Jersey: Prentice-Hall, 1972.

Glueck, William F. *Business Policy: Strategy Formation and Management Action.* Second Edition. New York, New York: McGraw-Hill Book Company, 1976.

Green, Paul E.; and Carroll, J. Douglas. *Mathematical Tools For Applied Multivariate Analysis.* New York, New York: Academic Press, 1976.

Green, Paul E.; and Tull, Donald S. *Research For Marketing Decisions.* Fourth Edition. Englewood Cliffs, New Jersey: Prentice-Hall, 1978.

_____. and Wind, Yoram. *Multiattribute Decisions In Marketing: A Measurement Approach.* Hinsdale, Ilinois: The Dryden Press, 1973.

Hartigan, John A. *Clustering Algorithms.* New York, New York: John Wiley and Sons, 1975.

Hays, William Lee. *Statistics.* New York, New York: Holt, Rinehart, and Winston, 1963.

Katz, Robert L. *Cases and Concepts in Corporate Strategy.* Englewood Cliffs, New Jersey: Prentice-Hall Inc., 1970.

Kolde, Endel Jakob. *International Business Enterprise.* Englewood Cliffs, New Jersey: Prentice-Hall Inc., 1968.

_____.*The Multinational Company.* Lexington, Massachusetts: D.C. Heath and Company, 1974.

Kotler, Philip. *Marketing Management: Analysis, Planning, and Control.* Englewood Cliffs, New Jersey: Prentice-Hall Inc., 1967.

Krooss, Herman E.; and Gilbert, Charles. *American Business History.* Englewood Cliffs, New Jersey: Prentice-Hall, 1972.

Learned, Edmund P.; Christensen, Charles R.; and Andrews, Kenneth R. *Problems of General Management-Business Policy.* Homewood, Illinois: Richard D. Irwin. 1961.

_____. et al. *Business Policy: Text and Cases.* Homewood, Illinois: Richard D. Irwin Inc., 1965.

McDonald, J. *The Game of Business.* Garden City, New York, New York: Doubleday and Company Inc., 1975.

McNichols, Thomas J. *Policymaking and Executive Action.* New York, New York: McGraw-Hill Book Company, 1977.

Miracle, Gordon E.; and Albaum, Gerald S. *International Marketing Management.* Homewood, Illinois: Richard D. Irwin Inc., 1970.

Nie, Norman H.; Hull, C. Hadlai; Jenkins, Jean G.; Steinbrenner, Karin; Bent, Dale H. *Statistical Package For The Social Sciences.* Second Edition. New York, New York: McGraw-Hill, 1975.

Porter, Michael E. *Interbrand Choice, Strategy, and Bilateral Market Power.* Cambridge, Massachusetts: Harvard University Press, 1976.

Rhys, D. G. *The Motor Industry: An Economic Survey.* London: Butterworth's Ltd., 1972.

Robinson, Richard D. *International Business Management: A Guide to Decision Making.* New York, New York: Holt, Rinehart, and Winston, Inc., 1973.

_____.*International Management.* New York, New York: Holt, Rinehart, and Winston, Inc., 1967.

Robock, Stefan H.; and Simmonds, Kenneth. *International Business and Multinational Enterprises.* Homewood, Illinois: Richard D. Irwin Inc., 1973.

Rumelt, Richard. *Strategy, Structure, and Economic Performance.* Cambridge, Mass.: Harvard University Press, 1974.

Schwendiman, John Snow. *Strategic and Long-Range Planning For The Multinational Corporation.* New York, New York: Praeger Publishers, 1973.

Smith, R. P. *Consumer Demand For Cars In The USA.* Cambridge, England: Cambridge University Press, 1975.

Statistical Abstract of the United States 1976. Washington, D. C.: Bureau of the Census, United States Department of Commerce, 1976.

Steiner, George A.; and Cannon, Warren M. *Multinational Corporate Planning.* New York, New York: The MacMillan Company, 1966.

Steiner, George A.; and Miner, John B. *Management Policy and Strategy: Text, Readings, and Cases.* New York, New York: MacMillan Publishing Co., 1977.

Tatsuoka, Maurice M. *Discriminant Analysis.* Champaign, Illinois: Institute For Personality and Ability Testing, 1970.

————. *Multivariate Analysis.* New York, New York: John Wiley & Sons Inc., 1971.

Thompson, Arthur A.; and Strickland, A. J., Ill. *Strategy and Policy: Concepts and Cases.* Dallas, Texas: Business Publications Inc., 1978.

Uyterhoeven, H.E.R.; Ackerman, R.W.; and Rosenblum, J.W. *Strategy and Organization: Text and Cases In General Management.* Homewood, Illinois: Richard D. Irwin Inc., 1973.

THESES AND DISSERTATIONS

Channon, Derek. "The Strategy and Structure of British Enterprise." unpublished DBA thesis, Harvard Business School, 1971.

Collings, Robert, "Scanning the Environment For Strategic Information." unpublished DBA thesis, Harvard Business School, 1968.

Darbyshire, Leslie. "The Competitive Position of Imported Automobiles in the American Market." unpublished DBA dissertation, Department of Finance, University of Washington, 1957.

Datta, Yudhishter. "Comparative Strategy and Performance of Firms in the U.S. Television Set Industry 1950–1960." unpublished Ph.D. dissertation, State University of New York at Buffalo, 1971.

Dyas, Gareth. "The Strategy and Structure of French Enterprise." unpublished DBA thesis, Harvard Business School, 1972.

Hunt, M.S. "Competition In The Major Home Appliance Industry, 1960–1970." unpublished Ph.D. dissertation, Business Economics Committee, Harvard University, May 1972.

Keegan, Warren. "Scanning the International Business Environment." unpublished DBA thesis, Harvard Business School, 1967.

Newman, H.H. "Strategic Groups and the Structure-Performance Relationship: A Study With Respect To The Chemical Process Industries." Ph.D. dissertation, Harvard University, December, 1973.

Pavan, Robert. "The Strategy and Structure of Italian Enterprise." unpublished DBA thesis, Harvard Business School, 1972.

Thanheiser, Heinz. "Strategy and Structure of German Enterprise." unpublished DBA thesis, Harvard Business School, 1972.

White, Lawrence Jay. "The American Automobile Industry In The Postwar Period." Ph.D. dissertation, Department of Economics, Harvard University, 1969.

JOURNALS

Abernathy, William J.; and Wayne, Kenneth. "Limits of the Learning Curve." *Harvard Business Review.* (September-October, 1974), pp. 109-119.

Ackoff, Russell L. "The Meaning of Strategic Planning." *McKinsey Quarterly*. (Summer 1966), pp. 48-61.

Ahers, F.C. "Negro, White Autobuying Behavior: New Evidence." *Journal of Marketing Research*. Vol. 5. (Aug. 1968), pp. 283-289.

Bell, G.D. "Self-Confidence: Persuasion in Car Buying." *Journal of Marketing Research*. Vol. 4, (Feb. 1967), pp. 46-52.

Bennett, Peter D.; and Mandell, Robert M. "Prepurchase Information Seeking Behavior of New Car Purchasers – The Learning Hypothesis." *Journal of Marketing Research*. Vol. VI, (Nov. 1969), pp. 430-433.

Bloom, Paul N.; and Kotler, Philip. "Strategies For High Market Share Companies." *Harvard Business Review*. (November-December, 1975), pp. 63-72.

Buzzell, Robert D. "Can You Standardize Multinational Marketing?" *Harvard Business Review*. (November–December 1968), pp. 102-113.

_____; Gale, Bradley T.; and Sultan, Ralph G.M. "Market Share: A Key to Profitability." *Harvard Business Review*. (January–February, 1975), pp. 97-106.

Catry, Bernard; and Chevalier, Michel. "Market Share Strategy and the Product Life Cycle." *Journal of Marketing*. (October, 1974), pp. 29-34.

Day, George S. "A Strategic Perspective On Product Planning." *Journal of Contemporary Business*. (Spring 1975a), pp. 1-35.

Frank, Ronald E.; and Green, Paul E. "Numerical Taxonomy In Marketing Analysis: A Review Article." *Journal of Marketing Research*. (February, 1968) pp. 83-98.

Fruhan, William E. "Pyrrhic Victories In Fights For Market Share." *Harvard Business Review*. (September-October, 1972), pp. 100-107.

Gale, Bradley T. "Market Share and Rate of Return." *Review of Economics and Statistics*. (November, 1972), pp. 412-423.

Grubb, Edward L.; and Hupp, Greg. "Perception of Self, Generalized Stereotypes, and Brand Selection." *Journal of Marketing Research*. Vol. 5, (Feb. 1968), pp. 58-63.

Keegan, Warren J. "Multinational Product Planning: Strategic Alternatives." *Journal of Marketing*. Vol. 33, (January, 1969), pp. 58-62.

Kotler, Philip. "Phasing Out Weak Products." *Harvard Business Review*. (March–April, 1965), pp. 107-118.

Lanzillotti, Robert F. "Multiple Products and Oligopoly Strategy: A Development of Chamberlin's Theory of Products." *Quarterly Journal of Economics*. (August, 1954), pp. 461-474.

Levitt, Theodore. "Improving Sales Through Product Augmentation." *European Business*. (April, 1969), pp. 5-12.

_____. "Marketing Myopia." *Harvard Business Review*. (July-August, 1960).

May, Frederick E. "Adaptive Behavior in Automobile Brand Choices." *Journal of Marketing Research*. Vol. VI, (February, 1969), pp. 62-65.

McGee, John S. "Economies of Size in Auto Body Manufacturing." *Journal of Law and Economics*. Vol. XVI, (October, 1973), pp. 239-273.

Reynolds, William H. "The Edsel, Ten Years Later." *Business Horizons*. (Fall 1967), pp. 39-46.

Schoeffler, Sidney; Buzzell, Robert D.; and Heany, Donald F. "Impact of Strategic Planning On Profit Performance." *Harvard Business Review*. (March–April, 1974), pp. 137-145.

Shuptrine, F.K.; and Samuelson, G. "Dimensions of Marital Roles in Consumer Decision Making: Revisited." *Journal of Marketing Research*. Vol. XIII, (Feb. 1976), pp. 87-91.

Sorenson, Ralph; and Wichmann, Ulrich. "How Multinationals View Marketing Standardization." *Harvard Business Review.* (May-June, 1975), pp. 38-54+.

Stuteville, John R. "The Buyer as a Salesman." *Journal of Marketing.* Vol. 32, (July, 1968), pp. 14-18.

Talley, Walter J. "Profiting From the Declining Product." *Business Horizons.* (Spring, 1964), pp. 77-84.

Tilles, Seymour. "How To Evaluate Corporate Strategy." *Harvard Business Review.* (July-August, 1963), pp. 111-121.

Vance, Jack O. "The Anatomy of a Corporate Strategy." *California Management Review.* (Fall, 1970). pp. 5-12.

Wall, Jerry. "What the Competition is Doing: Your Need to Know." *Harvard Business Review.* (November-December, 1974).

Wind, Yoram; and Claycamp, Henry J. "Planning Product Line Strategy: A Matrix Approach." *Journal of Marketing.* (January, 1976). pp. 2-9.

Wiseman, Frederick. "A Segmentation Analysis on Automobile Buyers During the New Model Year Transition Period." *Journal of Marketing.* Vol. 35, (April, 1971), pp. 42-49.

PROCEEDINGS AND COMPENDIA

Ansoff, H.I.; Declerck, R.P.; and Hayes, R.L. "From Strategic Planning To Strategic Management," *From Strategic Planning to Strategic Management.* New York, New York: John Wiley & Sons Inc. 1976, pp. 39-78.

Cooper, Arnold; DeMuzzio, E.; Hatten, K.; Hicks, E.; and Tock, D. "Strategic Responses To Technological Threats." *Proceedings, Academy of Management.* 1973, pp. 54-60.

Hofer, Charles W. "Some Preliminary Research on Patterns of Strategic Behavior." *Proceedings, Academy of Management.* 1973, pp. 46-54.

Jauch, Lawrence R.; Osborn Richard N.; and Glueck, William F. "Success in Large Business Organizations: The Environment-Strategy Connection." *Proceedings, Academy of Management.* 1977, pp. 113-117.

Murray, Edwin A. "Limitations on Strategic Choice." *Proceedings, Academy of Management.* 1976, pp. 140-144.

Newman, William H. "Strategic Considerations In Planning." *Readings in Management Strategy and Tactics.* John G. Hutchinson, editor. New York, New York: Holt, Rinehart, and Winston Inc., 171, pp. 72-79.

_____. "Strategy and Management Structure." *Proceedings, Academy of Management.* 1971.

Schendel, D.; and Patton, G.R. "An Empirical Study of Corporate Stagnation and Turnaround." *Proceedings, Academy of Management.* 1975, pp. 49-51.

Stuart, Fredric. ed. "Factors Affecting Determination of Market Shares In The American Automobile Industry." *Hofstra University Yearbook of Business.* Series 2, Volume 3, October, 1965.

Taylor, Ronald. "Age and Experience as Determinants of Managerial Information Processing and Decision-making Performance." *Academy of Management Journal.* Vol. XVIII, #1, 1975.

NEWSPAPERS, MAGAZINES AND PAMPHLETS

Abegglen, James C. "Perspectives: The Foreign Company in Japan–1977." Boston, Massachusetts: Boston Consulting Group, 1977.

_____. "Perspectives: Japan's Economy and the Foreign Company." Boston, Massachusetts: Boston Consulting Group, 1976.

Bylinski, Gene. "The Japanese Spies In Silicon Valley." *Fortune*, February 27, 1978, pp. 74-81.

"The Fortune Directory of the 500 Largest U.S. Industrial Corporations," Fortune, Vol. XCV, No. 5, May, 1977, p. 366.

"How the Japanese Blitzed the California Auto Market." *Forbes*, September 15, 1971, pp. 28-39.

"Import U.S. Sales by Years." *Ward Automotive Yearbook 1974.* p. 47.

"Japan – New Challenge to the U.S. in Autos." *U.S. News and World Report*, Vol. 65, August 5, 1968, pp. 63-64.

"Japan – Now Number 2 in Autos, Trucks and Going for Number 1." *U.S. News and World Report*, Vol. 68, June 1, 1970, pp. 42-43.

Klaw, Spencer. "The Soap Wars: A Strategic Analysis." *Fortune*, June 1963, pp. 123 +.

"New Car Sales Spurted by 12.5% in April From '76." *Wall Street Journal*, May 5, 1977, p. 7.

Rose, Sanford. "The Secret of Japan's Export Prowess." *Fortune*, January 30, 1978, pp. 56-63.

Index

BOWLING GREEN STATE UNIVERSITY
DISCARDED
LIBRARY

A113   0357654 7